Possum Hollow

Book 3

Possum Hollow

Book 3

Levi B. Weber

Herald
Press

Scottdale, Pennsylvania
Waterloo, Ontario

Library of Congress Cataloging-in-Publication Data
Weber, Levi B., 1911-
    Possum hollow / Levi B. Weber
       p. cm.
    ISBN 0-8361-9126-9 (bk. 1 : alk. paper)—ISBN 0-8361-9131-5
       (bk. 2 : alk. paper)—ISBN 0-8361-9144-7 (bk. 3 : alk.
       paper)—ISBN 0-8361-9145-5 (bk. 4 : alk. paper)
     1. Weber, Levi B., 1911- —Childhood and youth. 2. Farm
life—Pennsylvania—Lancaster County. 3. Farm life—
Virginia—Amelia County. 4. Mennonites—Pennsylvania—
Lancaster County—Biography. 5. Amelia County (Va.)—
Biography. 6. Lancaster County (Pa.)—Biography. I. Title.
CT275.W3526 A3 2001
974.8'15044—dc21   00-053940

The paper used in this publication is recycled and meets the
minimum requirements of American National Standard for
Information Sciences—Permanence of Paper for Printed
Library Materials, ANSI Z39.48-1984.

Scripture is from the King James Version.

POSSUM HOLLOW, BOOK 3
Copyright © 2002 by Herald Press, Scottdale, Pa. 15683
    Published simultaneously in Canada by Herald Press,
    Waterloo, Ont. N2L 6H7. All rights reserved
Library of Congress Control Number: 00-053940
International Standard Book Number: 0-8361-9144-7
Printed in the United States of America
Book and cover design by Sandra Johnson
Cover art and possum motif by Joy Dunn Keenan
Inside illustrations by Ken Stetz

10 09 08 07 06 05 04 03 02   10 9 8 7 6 5 4 3 2 1

To order or request information, please call
1-800-759-4447 (individuals); 1-800-245-7894 (trade).
Website: www.mph.org

To my wife,
June Elizabeth Weber

Without the encouragement I received from June, I would never have written *Possum Hollow*. When she heard me tell stories to the children, she would often say, "Why don't you write about it?"

She knew it wouldn't be easy because she had written a book, *The Tribe of Jacob*, stories about her mother's family of fifteen children growing up in the Shenandoah Valley of Virginia.

June was always glad to read my manuscripts and suggest corrections or changes before they were given to the typist. Thank you, June!

Contents

Preface

A pleasant Sunday afternoon found me sitting on the floor of the front porch, resting my back against the wall. I was thinking about an argument two boys were having about horses and automobiles. This happened outside after church one Sunday morning.

Several weeks earlier, a man had been driving his car too fast around a corner, and he landed in a cornfield. The ground was soft, and he had to get a horse to pull the car out. One boy said, "That proves horses will always be needed." The other boy said, "Tractors and other machinery will do away with horses. Cowboys will soon be riding motorcycles."

As far as I was concerned, their arguments didn't prove anything. We used to go around in horses and buggies, but now we had both horses and automobiles. Tractors might take the place of horses, but the idea of cowboys on motorcycles was just plain dumb. I remembered the big old steam traction engine coming to steam our tobacco bed. Horses and machines would both be needed.

My daydreaming was interrupted when Helen came through the front door beside me. She was holding a book of poetry. Looking out over the fields she said, "Oh, isn't it a beautiful day! Everybody ought to be happy." Opening her book, she read:

> *So, here has been dawning*
> *Another blue day;*
> *Think, wilt thou let it*
> *Slip useless away?*
> *Out of Eternity*
> *This new day was born;*
> *Into Eternity*
> *At night will return.*

Closing the book, she walked out to the picket fence and looked up the narrow country road toward Webster. Shaded by large trees on either side, it was like a path through a park.

She stood there a moment and then said, "Levi, come on; let's walk up and take a look at the school. I'm going to be teaching there soon."

—*Levi B. Weber*
Newport News, Virginia

Summer Music

1

Esther and Buffalo Bill

As soon as Helen came home from Millersville State Normal School (MSNS) for the summer, she began to teach me things she had learned in her botany class about plants and flowers.

Sometimes on Sunday afternoons, she would take Esther and me walking in the woods, looking for wild flowers. She would point out plants and flowers we hadn't noticed before. The woods became something special, more than just a place to play.

Starting along the edge of the woods, following the stream, we found cress and other plants that grew by the water. We tramped as far as the fence at Weidman's woods, then turned right, coming to a little marsh no bigger than our living room. An invisible spring kept it fresh all year.

When we approached, tiny frogs jumped behind clumps of marsh grass. Wasps and birds were often there, getting mud for nests. Skunk cabbage grew around the edges of the marsh. Ranging here and there, we found dogstooth violets, star grass, arbutus, anemones, Solomon's seal, and many other flowers that were new to us.

We were allowed to walk in Weidman's woods, so we included that in our nature walks. In her little book, Helen listed as many as fifteen different plant specimens.

The woods always reminded me of scenes from *Robin Hood* or *Two Little Savages*. One area was especially enticing. Entering from where the dam used to be, we came to a natural lane about four feet wide, lined with small trees and shrubs. Along the lane, I used to break off twigs and chew on the bark. One kind tasted like peppermint and another like wintergreen.

I called the little trail Lovers' Lane. I got the idea from an old wartime ballad:

> Smile the while you kiss me sad adieu,
> When the clouds roll by I'll come to you,
> Then the skies will seem more blue
> Down in lovers' lane, my dear-ee,
> Wedding bells will ring so merril-ee,
> Every tear will be a memor-ee,
> So wait and pray each night for me
> Till we meet again.
>   —Richard Whiting, composer

I planned to build a little shed there sometime, right between the lane and the creek. To be ready for the project, I had collected a pile of old boards and stashed them underneath the bushes. My little shed would be my headquarters, just like the shanty in *Two Little Savages.*

Esther and I had thoroughly read all our books and were up to date with the *Youth's Christian Companion* and the *Rural New Yorker.* Then one day she came to me with what appeared to be a large sheet of paper from a magazine. "Let's go for a walk," she said. When we had secret things to talk about, we would "go for a walk."

We went around behind the house to the hillside meadow, sat down together under the big apple tree, and examined the paper. It was a list of many books that could be bought for only ten cents each. There were certain rules to go by. No purchase for less than fifty cents, and there was a packaging and mailing charge of at least fifty cents.

Esther had it all figured out. "If we each buy two books, a one-dollar bill is sure to be enough." We would use money we earned from our market commissions. I gave Esther fifty cents, and she supplied the dollar.

We had always ordered from Sears & Roebuck before, so this was something new. After we chose our books, Esther would write up the order, and I would sneak it out to the mailbox. We selected our books from a section called "True Life Stories of America."

Esther chose *Buffalo Bill Cody: A True Story of the West* and *Buffalo Bill: A Man on the Range.*

My selections were *Peck's Bad Boy: A Real Story of a Real Boy* and *Peck's Bad Boy Goes West.*

I always got the mail, so when *our* package came, hiding the books was no problem. Esther made the

whole thing seem like a mystery. On Sunday afternoon we each took one of our books and went for a
walk to the big apple tree. There we sat down to read

what for some reason had become a hush-hush matter.

Esther was reading *Buffalo Bill Cody*, and I had selected *Peck's Bad Boy Goes West*. I could tell Peck's Bad Boy was no Robin Hood. I was just at the place where he had jumped a freight train and was riding West in an empty boxcar. He was fighting hunger by eating axle grease from the freight-car journal boxes.

Just then Esther slapped her book on the ground as though she was mad. I thought maybe Buffalo Bill had gotten killed.

She moaned in a low voice, deep with shame, "Why, these are dime novels!"

In our church circles, dime novels were not suitable reading. Just a few weeks earlier, at a Sunday school meeting, a speaker had declared, "Our nation is being ruined by movies and dime novels."

Esther said, "I should have known what they were since they only cost a dime." She began to sniff, and tears ran down her cheeks. "We'll have to destroy the books."

We got the other two books and returned to the apple tree. Right below us was the large drainage ditch, packed with old tree branches to reduce erosion. We tore the books into small pieces and stuck them deep under the brush, where they couldn't be seen. She warned me, "Don't tell anyone." Then we left.

She was still crying. I pitied her because she always tried to do things right, but this time she missed it.

2

My Organ Lessons

I liked to play around on the old organ we kept in the storeroom at the end of the house. Mama had bought it at a household sale one time because no one else had bid on it. The auctioneer knocked it off for her ten-dollar bid.

The organ was too worn-out to have a place in the parlor, where most people kept their instruments. At one time it surely must have occupied an important spot, with its elegant scrollwork and lampstands. Above the keyboard was a row of stops bearing names: octave coupler, vox humana, flute, and diapason. There were also two knee-operated swell levers below the keyboard, to control the volume.

Singing around the piano was a regular activity when families visited together on Sunday afternoons. Usually someone would play the piano while each of us sang his particular part. Some people had player pianos. The playing was automatic. A roll of properly punched paper was placed in a special place, and the piano played by itself. The words of the song were printed on the margin of the roll so we didn't even need a songbook. Someone had to pump the pedals to make the machinery work; that was all that was necessary.

I couldn't really play the organ like Miss Young did at school; I just picked around on the keys. I knew about notes and things like that from singing at church. I soon was able to find the notes for simple songs in the key of C or the key of F. The key of F used only one black key. I would practice on hymns written in those keys. I just pressed the keys with whatever fingers were closest.

Once when I was playing around with the song "Sun of My Soul," I noticed how the harmony flowed and how the chords seemed to keep reaching for the next one until the final chord. Some chords seemed especially anxious to be resolved in the next one, such as when the black key was involved. I usually played with the vox humana stop pulled out. That made the music sound wavy, with vibrato, as some ladies sang in church. Helen said *vox humana* was Latin for human voice.

Mama knew I liked to play on the organ, so she arranged for me to take some music lessons. Dad said, "You should stay with the organ and not take piano lessons." I knew the keyboards were the same, so I didn't say anything. Mama set it up for me to take lessons with Mrs. Doster at Brunnerville.

My first lesson was on a Saturday afternoon. I went two miles up the road on foot. My lesson would cost fifty cents, and I was to buy a book for seventy-five cents. I was used to walking and didn't mind distance. I was glad there were no dogs on the way since I was still afraid of them.

Mrs. Doster met me at the door. I wiped my shoes on the doormat and went in. As expected, she had a piano and not an organ.

The lessons began well. She showed me how to place my fingers on the keys, crossing my thumb and all that. Next she explained the lettering of the scale and the clefs. It didn't seem hard. The fingering exercises gave me the most trouble. I preferred to just move my hands around and strike with whichever finger was closest.

The girls were glad I was taking lessons. Eva asked me, "Do you remember when I wanted an organ down south in Amelia, and didn't get one?"

When Franklin heard about my lessons, he laughed and said, "I guess when Mama heard my playing, she knew something had to be done."

Esther didn't say anything about my music lessons. Ever since the dime novel thing, she had seemed rather quiet, not talking much.

When Mrs. Doster began to drill me on identifying the letters of the scale, I got into trouble. We would sit together on the piano bench, with the exercise book on the piano. She would place the tip of her pencil on a certain line or space and ask me to name its letter. I never got it right. I would say what I knew was right, but she always said it was something else.

Finally she would give up and say, "Levi, you just have to study that some more until you have it."

But no amount of study seemed to help.

I didn't like Mrs. Doster. I knew she must have called Mama because one day Mama quietly said to me, "Levi, I guess we are going to stop the lessons. But you are playing the organ better than you did before."

So I just went back to pumping our old leaky organ, hunting the keys like I used to do. I forgot about running up and down the scale, crossing my thumb at the fourth note, and so on.

One day while sitting at the organ, thinking back over my times with Mrs. Doster, I suddenly had an idea. I thought carefully about her pencil point and how she had always said I was wrong when I wasn't. She hadn't wanted the letter of the line or space *at* her pencil point; she had wanted the note directly *above* it!

It was too late to set it right with Mrs. Doster. The lessons were over. I didn't even try to explain it to Mama. But I was mad at Mrs. Doster. She was the top teacher at the Brunnerville two-room school. She should have caught on to the fact that I was calling her pencil point correctly.

Esther hadn't taken much interest in my short run with music. She had something else going on in her mind that soon came out. She confided in Mama and Dad that she wanted to join the church and become a church member. Esther said there was another girl her age attending the Lititz church who wanted to join, too. Dad said he would talk to our preacher about it.

I was used to seeing people join the church because of getting stirred up at revival meetings. But revival meetings would not be coming until early fall. I figured that Esther must have been able to understand things without hearing what the visiting preachers had to say.

Esther and the other girl met several times with the preacher and the bishop. They conducted a baptismal service one Sunday morning at Lititz Church. In the sermon the bishop spoke well of the young ladies, who in their early years were choosing to come to the Lord, even without the urging that was so often necessary.

After being baptized, Esther was happier again and began to be more involved with visiting among other girls her age. She seemed more grown-up. When school started in the fall, she would leave Webster and be going to Lititz High.

3

Music and Romance

Helen often sang while she sewed and sometimes would hum while she was reading. Back when she was still in high school, her friend Hulda Ginder would visit over the weekend. They often sang together as they washed the dishes. Hulda's alto voice gave a romantic blend to songs like "Love's Old Sweet Song."

One Sunday afternoon some of Helen's friends dropped in to visit. One of the girls brought along her ukulele, a little instrument with four strings. The uke had become a fad. It was easy to play, and three or four simple chords could be formed with the left hand while the right hand strummed the strings with a felt pick.

The group began to sing well-known songs while the girl walked around, holding her ukulele close and strumming the accompaniment. Since the uke was supposed to come from Hawaii, they wanted to sing the "Aloha `Oe" song. The girl said, "Wait, I have to tune up again." She began to tune the uke by ear, matching a little vocal ditty, "Uk-u-le-lee."

One of the boys said, "Are you sure you have the right word? I do it different."

She handed him the uke and said, "I didn't know you played. Here, see if you can tune it better." I could tell she was peeved.

He took it and softly stroked the strings. Then, one at a time, he struck each string, loudly singing, "My—dog—has—fleas." When everyone stopped laughing, they tried to sing "Aloha `Oe." It began with a dramatic image: "Proudly swept the rain cloud o'er the cliff."

The song went on, interspersed with Hawaiian words, and finally finishing with—

Farewell to thee, farewell to thee,
Thou charming one who dwells among the flowers.
One fond embrace before we now depart,
Until we me—eet again.
    —Queen Lili`uokalani

The "uke girl" (the name I gave her) was the only one who knew it. She smiled her way through the whole thing, and then the singing was over.

The ukulele caught Helen's fancy, and she finally bought one for herself. So we all had many chances to hear more uke music.

One day Eva and Helen gave us all a big surprise. They had pooled their money and bought a Victrola. It would be delivered the coming Saturday afternoon. Victrolas were the popular thing, and many people had them in their parlors.

Some models were vertical, with a record cabinet below and a turntable above, hidden under a hinged cover. Another kind was horizontal, with the record cabinet and player side by side. Eva said theirs was the horizontal kind and was a nice piece of furniture.

One of our neighbors still had an old Victor Talking Machine. It had a big horn hovering over a base that held the playing equipment. The records were cylinders with grooves, which made the music. It was counted as furniture.

"When You and I Were Young, Maggie" was on one of their records. I liked the funny ones about "Uncle Josh and the Lightning Rod" and "Uncle Josh and the Shutter." Uncle Josh said all his words wrong, mixed up his sentences, and never did anything right.

The Victrola was delivered to our place on Saturday, as scheduled. Set in place and carefully gone over with furniture polish, it gave the parlor an elegance it never had before. Then Helen brought from her room a bunch of records she must have been buying in advance. After she and Eva had placed them in order in the cabinet, she said we would play some of them in the evening after supper.

We begged her, "Play just one now." So she selected "Jerusalem the Golden," sung by the Trinity Choir with orchestra. It was so good that we begged for more.

Eva gave in, and we gathered around while she and Helen selected several more to play:

"One Sweetly Solemn Thought," a hymn
"Oh, Promise Me," a love song
"I Love You Truly," a love song
"The Hallelujah Chorus," from Handel's *Messiah*
"In the Gloaming, Oh, My Darling," a love song

Before we finished, Dad came in and sat down to listen a while. He didn't like "The Hallelujah Chorus." He said, "It sounds like a bunch of dogs barking." He liked the old hymns.

"In the Gloaming" was a sad song, such as a soprano solo with orchestra:

In the gloaming, oh, my darling!
When the lights are dim and low,
And the quiet shadows falling,
Softly come and softly go.
When the winds are sobbing faintly
With a gentle, unknown woe,
Will you think of me, and love me,
As you did once long ago?

In the gloaming, oh, my darling!
Think not bitterly of me!
Tho' I pass'd away in silence,
Left you lonely, set you free.
For my heart was crush'd with longing,
What had been could never be;
It was best to leave you thus, dear,
Best for you and best for me.
            —text by Meta Orred

I was deeply touched by the sad romance. What had happened? What had gone wrong? The girls didn't know what the story was about; it was just a nice song. But "In the Gloaming" kept playing over and over in my mind. I didn't like sad romances. The stories I liked best ended happily, maybe amid beautiful flowers and under a lovely moon.

4

Singing School

Again, summer was a busy time. Everyone was home except Helen. After a short stay, she went back to MSNS for a summer term that would complete her two-year requirement for a teacher's certificate. That's why she would be teaching at Webster this year. Eva would be teaching at Sun Hill School near Manheim. She was glad to be nearer home instead of at Brecknock, over near Terre Hill.

Alongside the summer work and other activities, I sneaked enough time to finally build my little house in the woods down by the stream. I brought an old saw and hammer from Dad's toolbox and kept them under the pile of boards I had collected for this project. I filled an empty molasses kettle with eight-penny nails and covered it with a board.

I had never liked to work with tools and was not very good with them. Dad and the rest of our family were skilled with their hands, but I was clumsy with carpentry and mechanical work. They just accepted me as I was and never teased me. This time, I set out to do a neat job and was determined that it would be special.

Finally I finished the house. It was about five feet square. I had tried hard, and it was almost perfectly square. The roof was not quite head high, so I had to stoop inside. The walls were made of old boards standing upright and nailed together onto horizontal cleats.

The shed roof was made of the same kind of boards. It leaked a little, so I tried using some old putty to fill the cracks, but water still dripped through in a hard rain. For the doorway, I simply left out three boards from the wall. I made a desk by fastening three boards along one side. My desk chair was an old milk stool.

When it was finished, I brought some little wooden cigar boxes and tin cans for storing my special things, such as several pencils and some crayons. I fixed a secret place under the desk for an old composition book Eva had given me.

This now was my real headquarters. From here, my imagination took me, like Robin Hood, through the forest to right the wrongs "wrought by the evil sheriff."

When I showed my house to Esther, she said, "This isn't a house. It's a shed because it has a shed roof." Then she sat on the milk stool and began talking about how she would be going to Lititz High School in a few weeks.

She would be a freshman. It had been arranged for her to board with Ephraim and Millie Eby. They were an elderly couple we knew, living near the school. Esther would help in the house to pay for her keep. Millie was the lady who wouldn't take the birdhouse Franklin had wanted to give her because, as she said, "It would draw birds that would dirty my porch."

During the summer, we had a singing school at Hess's Church. We met each Saturday evening for six weeks. Singing schools were held in different churches from time to time. Song leaders would introduce new songs and teach people to sing in four-part harmony.

This year we were going to learn selections out of a new book called *Life Songs* (1916). Some of the churches had *Life Songs* as extras in the songbook racks of their benches. Hess's didn't want to spend the money, so we each bought our own.

We enjoyed singing school. Our teacher was Davy Wenger, a robust man with a ringing baritone voice. Our textbook was *The Vocal Gem—Containing Rudiments of Music, Voice Culture, Graded Lessons, and Songs.* Davy arranged the class of about forty people in four sections: soprano, alto, tenor, and bass. The children just sat together and sang soprano.

There were four men and several women who always sang in a continuous monotone, but yet they would select one of the four parts and try to do their part. At home we would talk about it. Esther said, "They're tone deaf and think they're actually singing their special part."

"I think they probably can hear the four-part harmony," Franklin said, "but can't carry a tune."

I didn't know the answer. I just knew they sang

freely and seemed to enjoy it as much as the rest of us.

I was excited about being in the singing school and especially liked the *Life Songs*. The first one we learned was on page 59, "Meet Him in the Morning." It was in the key of C and in 6/4 time. That meant there were six beats per measure, with one beat per quarter note.

We were taught about beating time with a hand for leading in singing. I knew that sometime when I was grown-up, I would lead singing. I would imagine myself standing before an audience of five hundred people and, just like Davy Wenger, be leading a favorite song. I could hear the ringing harmony as we sang, "Bringing in the Sheaves."

Then I began to be worried about something. Suppose I was a monotone and my family was too nice to tell me. I thought about how sometimes the person sitting next to me sang in that dull, single pitch. Maybe I was tone deaf, too. I knew the four-part harmony and fooled with the organ, so maybe I was all right.

Then one of the older men who led singing in the church made me forget my worry. He came to me after church one Sunday and said, "Levi, I heard you singing today. You have a fine voice. You could be a chorister someday."

My worries were over. I didn't have to risk asking Esther or Franklin whether I could sing.

5

The Picnic

The Eby family was well known. They owned and operated a shoe factory in Lititz. They were also known and appreciated in our church for their participation in teaching and singing activities.

The Eby brothers—Frank, Elmer, and Elias—had rich baritone and tenor voices. Their sister, Mrs. Elam Risser, was one of our special altos. The Snyder and Hershey families were also gifted singers. My favorite high soprano was Ada Leed.

Elmer Eby would usually select hymns with flowing rhythm and harmony rather than those with jumpy refrains. One of his favorites was "In Thy Holy Place."

In Thy holy place we bow,
Perfumes sweet to heaven rise,
While our golden censers glow
With the fire of sacrifice.

Saints low bending, prayers ascending,
Holy lips and hands implore;—
Faith believing and receiving
Grace from Him whom we adore.
　　　—text by S. F. Coffman, music by J. D. Brunk

In the early days when we first began attending our young people's meetings, four of the men had formed a male quartet. I remember one of their songs, "For the Man of Galilee." At the same meeting, two young women, Suely Enk from Lancaster and Edna Snyder from Lititz, were singing in a duet.

We all enjoyed their "special singing," but it was soon discontinued. The Bishop Board saw special singing as a form of display. It could also open the door to other unacceptable forms of worship. Our congregational singing still remained a great source of inspiration.

One weekend Esther brought home some information about the Ebys I hadn't heard before. Ephraim and Millie Eby's daughter, Martha, was the wife of Clayton F. Yake, editor of the *Youth's Christian Companion,* published at Scottdale, in western Pennsylvania. The same establishment also published the children's magazines *Words of Cheer* and *Beams of Light.*

Clayton and Martha had come home to the Ebys for a short vacation. Clayton brought along a big pile of paperwork. He would spread it out on the table, laboring over his editorial submissions. Esther said Martha had more of a vacation than her husband.

Frank Eby's daughter, Anna, was one of Esther's friends. She was among the young people invited to go with us on our annual picnic, in a meadow by the Conestoga Creek. Our long-body Ford truck with its roof and curtains could carry up to a dozen people. Dad and Mama were our hosts and chaperones.

When we arrived at our location, we set up camp. Using curtains and poles, the girls erected a small dressing area. The boys were wearing their pants and shirts over their swimming suits. They didn't need a dressing room to remove their clothes.

There was swimming, rowboating, and games. A folding table was opened to hold the huge lunch, with plenty of lemonade. The picnic lasted till four o'clock.

On the way home, we dropped people off at their homes. When we reached home, it was time for the evening chores. Our supper was picnic leftovers.

It had been a good day.

The Fall with
Sister Teacher

6

Helen Teaches at Webster

After summer vacation, our family became separated again, as usual. This September it was a little different. Helen would be at home and teaching at Webster. Esther would be away, living at Lititz. Eva was going to be teaching at Sun Hill and boarding in the home of the Jacob Carper family.

This three-way switch among the girls changed the relationships at home. Esther was no longer the "big girl" at home. That pleased me. Helen would have that place now. Helen was always special to me back in the old days when she would read to me and explain things.

The rest of us now at home were Franklin—age sixteen, Betty—age five, little Henry—age two, and I was ten years old.

Franklin worked at grown-up things, and Betty

sometimes helped to dry the dishes while standing on a little stool. Sometimes Mama would let her help to bake. She gave her some extra dough and let her work it out, making little cutout cookies covered with sugar sprinkles. Helen helped when she could but was usually busy with school things.

My job was helping with the milking and the cream separator, feeding and watering the chickens, and gathering the eggs.

Chickens had always interested me. When I worked with them, I began to notice hens that had their own way of doing things. Some were bossy, and others were timid. I noticed that they usually wanted to roost at the same place and waited at certain nests for their turn to lay their eggs. All of our chickens were white leghorns, but the special habits of some were obvious.

I gathered eggs at noon and in the evening. By noontime, the hens had already deposited a lot of eggs in the nests. Some hens were laying eggs in the nests, and others were standing by, waiting their turn. Sometimes a mean old hen would peck my hand when I reached under her for the eggs.

The process of egg laying fascinated me. The large white eggs were squeezed out with little effort. The hens' cackling (bragging?) while laying eggs made the whole process appear to be a happy situation. Occasionally there would be a big double-yolk egg. The hen didn't seem to mind.

One time when I said something to Mama about egg-laying, she didn't make any comment. The next day Dad told me in an offhand way, "Just gather the eggs and don't watch the hens laying their eggs." I knew I must have crossed over from proper interests into the forbidden mysteries of life.

Each week I received a little spending money for my work. One Sunday when my friend Paul Huber was visiting, he went with me to gather the eggs. He carried the basket while I gathered. At a certain high point of our conversation about his new bicycle, he accidentally dropped the basket. There was a big mess. All except twelve of the eggs were broken.

The chickens instantly gathered around and began cleaning up the sloppy mess. We took what was left to the basement. After Paul had left, I explained the accident to Dad, who said, "You're responsible for those eggs." That week I didn't get my spending money.

Now that school had started, I no longer gathered eggs at noon. I ran home from school to eat dinner (lunch) and then back again in time to play for the rest of noon recess.

I knew I was going to like Helen for a teacher. She had always helped me to learn things at home. Since the school was only a few hundred yards from home, she could walk, even with her slight limp, the result of her childhood paralysis. I didn't walk along with her. She started a little earlier to unlock and get the school open. She carried along her book bag and lunch box.

The first day after the bell rang, we were seated and she stood before us with the roll-call book. She introduced herself and said we should call her "Miss Weber" or just "Teacher." Since she was local, we already knew well in advance who she was.

Then she asked us to line up along the outer aisle

while she called our names and gave us our seats. The little ones were up front at the small desks, and the older ones back farther had larger desks. There were seventeen pupils, from six to fifteen years old.

After this, Teacher conducted the standard opening. She read a short Psalm from the *Bible*, after which we all repeated the Lord's Prayer and gave the flag salute. Next she had two of the big girls help pass out the books, pencils, and tablets.

When we were all settled, she looked at us and said, "I'm so proud to be teaching at Webster. I am not going to make a lot of rules. Good students know how to behave. We are all going to be honest and trust each other.

"If you raise a hand, I'll come to your desk to see what you want. But if your pencil needs sharpening, you don't have to raise your hand for permission. I'll trust you to just go quietly to the sharpener."

She also said something else rather unusual: "As we go on in the school year and problems come up, we'll talk things over first, and then together we'll try to make rules. That way those rules will be *your* rules."

Everyone was pleased and excited. At recess we talked about it. One of the boys suggested, "Maybe we can make a rule for taking a holiday sometime."

Clarence Weidman, one of the wise older boys, said, "That would not be a rule. That would be more like a law, and laws were made by the gov'ment."

The girls talked about making rules to keep the boys from making fun of them.

One of the first problems we discussed was about two boys who were always fighting at recess. Two girls were always tattling to the teacher about it. I didn't know what Helen said to them, but the two boys didn't fight any more, and the tattling stopped.

School was getting to be fun. I liked it.

7

Abstruse

It was a lovely Sunday afternoon. We were on our way to Weaverland Mennonite Church where Preacher I. B. Good would be speaking about "Peace in the World," one of his favorite subjects. He was a well-educated minister who at one time had been the principal of Terre Hill High School. He was also a counselor for young men during the stress of the great World War (I). This would be one of a series of sermons he had been giving in different churches.

After driving through gently rolling farm country, we finally arrived at the church. Finding a place to park was not easy because the lot was full. Through the open windows, we could hear the sound of singing.

As we entered the crowded building, the only place left to sit was near the back. Esther and Helen found a spot among the ladies, while Dad, Franklin, and I crowded into the men's side. The moderator and I. B. Good were seated on the bench behind the pulpit, along with several other visiting preachers.

When the singing was finished, the moderator stood up and gave a short introduction: "Brother I. B. Good is well-known and respected in the church and community. May we all be blessed by what we hear today." After offering a short prayer, he took his seat.

Brother Good spoke in an even voice, pronouncing his words distinctly. His message was one of hope for a time of world peace. He pointed out passages of Scripture that promised a time when wars would be a thing of the past. "Indeed, this late great destructive war could well be the war to end all wars."

He spoke further of a new spirit of hope and quietness. The great interest in sports and other "non-productive" use of time was on the wane. "We don't see young men playing ball in the meadows on Sunday afternoons anymore." He spoke of a time that was wonderful and yet somewhat mysterious—profound, but so abstruse. As he pronounced the word *abstruse*, he paused, as if to give the audience time for reflection.

We returned home again through the quiet countryside, talking about the things we had heard. "The message was full of hope," Dad said. He read the Bible a lot, and he was our Sunday school superintendent.

He quoted a passage from the Bible: "They shall beat their swords into plowshares and their spears into pruning hooks. Nation shall not rise up against nation; neither shall they study war any more."

Preacher Good had used a lot of big words that I couldn't understand. I was especially impressed by the word *abstruse*. Just as I was about to ask what it meant, we rounded a bend and there, in a meadow, was a bunch of boys playing baseball—on Sunday!

"Look!" Esther cried out. "Remember what the preacher said about baseball?"

Dad just said, "Let's think about the good things we heard and not put a damper on the message by starting an argument. We benefit more by talking about good things than by finding fault at every opportunity."

The conversation changed to school matters. "The Eby home, where I'm staying, is very quiet," Esther said. "On our farm, there's always something going on, and there are people to talk to."

I didn't want to talk about school. It would have been a little awkward since Helen was my teacher. I did say, "Everybody seems glad to have Helen for our teacher."

While doing my Sunday evening chores, I kept going over the big words the preacher had used. I knew words like *prophecy* and *kingdom*. They were not new to me. We were always talking about words at home. I don't know why the word *abstruse* stuck in my mind. I kept seeing the look on the preacher's face when he said it.

One time when I heard Eva and Helen talking about words, Eva laughed and said, "Some words are their own definition." Maybe this word was one of those. Anyhow, I was afraid to ask what it meant.

Back at school on Monday, my thoughts turned to other things. Helen told us older pupils, "Each of you are going to make a scrapbook." She held up a composition book like the one she used.

"The scrapbook will be like a diary," she said. "You can write or draw anything you think is interesting, such as a special song or poem you've learned during the year. You can cut and paste designs from colored craft paper. Or you may draw with crayons."

After explaining things and answering questions, she gave each of us a composition book. I took mine and, just as she had instructed, I printed some identification on the first page—what she called the flyleaf:

Levi B. Weber
Sixth Reader
1922

I worked a long time before I came up with a design for the cover. First I pasted a square piece of brown craft paper over the entire front cover, to hide the advertising. Then I made four little squares of green craft paper. I placed one in each corner of the cover.

That left an open space in the center for the title. Measuring carefully with my ruler, right in the center I printed with my red crayon, "Scrap Book."

8

Flies and More Flies

Flies were a part of life. Just like the leaves on trees, they came in the spring and disappeared in the fall. But unlike leaves that were beautiful and made life pleasant, flies were a pest and spoiled things. There were all kinds of flies: houseflies, horseflies, bluebottle flies, fruit flies, and hoards of others. Flies were everywhere and in every situation. Someone once joked that when Adam and Eve ate the apple, fruit flies ate the core.

People had all kinds of remedies and defenses for flies, such as sticky flypaper in square sheets or in ribbons hanging from the ceiling. There were all kinds of flyswatters and even fly chasers that looked like feather dusters.

Fly poison was available in several forms. Ordinary poison usually came in squares of dark gray paper, to be placed in old pie plates with water.

Daisy Fly Killer was designed to be used in the parlor or living room. It consisted of a round, flat container about six inches in diameter and one-half inch high. It contained the poison. Daisies were painted on the cover. In the center of each daisy was a soft, round wick that drew up the poison. I guess the flies were supposed to think they were feasting on flowers.

Mama didn't use fly poison. She didn't like finding dead flies deposited around on the tables and floors. This was especially bad in the kitchen, around food and cooking. Mama was skilled with flyswatters, and there was always one close by. Our fly problem wasn't too bad because Dad had provided the house with good screen doors and screens for the windows.

Fall was approaching. Days were not quite as hot, and nights were getting a bit chilly. The fly season was also on the decline. When nights were chilly, large numbers of flies would collect on the wall outside the kitchen door, where it was warm. During the night they got stiff from the cold and couldn't fly. In the morning, Mama would sweep them down into the dustpan and deposit them in the kitchen stove. I liked the odd smell of burning flies.

When Eva came home on weekends, she would tell us about the Carper families. She was boarding with the Jacob Carper family. They had several children, with the oldest a boy my age. Jacob had a younger brother, Henry, who also had a farm.

The rest of Jacob's family of origin lived together in Lititz. They were the old widowed mother; two older sisters, Lizzie and Ellen; and a single brother,

Reuben. He was in his early twenties and had a job in the lumberyard at Lititz.

Reuben was not at home. With three of his friends, he had gone way out west to the state of Washington, to pick apples. The young men were staying at Wenatchee in the apple country. They had driven all the way in Reuben's Buick touring car. When the apple season was over, they would be returning.

Eva had a good opinion of the Carper families. She spoke of the nice farms where Jacob and Henry were living with their own families. After their father had died, the rest of the family had settled in his home in Lititz. Eva hadn't seen Reuben yet, but Mrs. Jacob Carper had shown his picture to her.

Reuben would soon be returning to live with the family at Lititz and to return to his job. Whenever Eva talked about teaching at Sun Hill or about things where she was boarding, she would somehow manage to say something about Reuben. I began wondering if she was hoping a friendship might develop.

At Webster School, things were going well. Helen had placed a small reading table and two chairs up front, on the left end of the platform, just below a shelf of miscellaneous books. When we had finished our lessons, we were allowed to go to the table, look over the shelf, and select a book to read.

At recess I went forward and looked at the reading material. Most were old books someone had no doubt given to get rid of. One, however, looked interesting. The title was *In Freedom's Cause*.

I began to read it at the table whenever I had

time. It was about Sir William Wallace and Robert Bruce, both famous warriors who struggled against England for the freedom of Scotland. The book had a full-page picture of Robert Bruce standing boldly upright, holding his sword with its point on the ground. Below the picture were Robert's words: "I am done with weeping." His friend William Wallace had been captured and executed. Now he, Robert the Bruce, would fight on for freedom.

I liked the new songs we were beginning to sing, the stories Helen would tell, and the poems we memorized. One of the songs was a simple children's song, but I liked it anyway. It was about "Little Boy Blue."

> Across the meadowland sweet with morn,
> I hear the sound of a silver horn.
> (Echo) I hear the sound of a silver horn.
>
> Little Boy Blue with heart so true,
> I will arise and go with you.
> (Echo) I will arise and go with you.

We were taught to sing the echo softly, just like an echo.

My first scrapbook entry was about "Little Boy Blue." I took a piece of blue craft paper and cut out a silhouette of a little boy with a strawhat. I pasted it on one side of the sheet. At the top I pasted a cutout of a little horn, leaving just enough room to carefully print the "Little Boy Blue" song.

I was getting something in school I had never realized before. School was becoming more than just

learning multiplication tables and rules of grammar.
Maybe there was more to grammar than just words.
Sometime I would try to write a poem, I decided.

9

A Bad Idea

The corn was all husked and the fodder stacked behind the barn. The corn ears were in the cribs, and the field turnips stowed in the old tobacco cellar. Big yellow pumpkins could be seen out in the empty cornfield. In two weeks it would be Halloween.

When cold weather began, we stopped going barefoot. Since I was still a boy, I wore knee pants and long stockings. Everyday shoes were designed to come up a little above the ankles. The shoestrings were threaded through holes except toward the top, where hooks were added. Girls' shoes were different, and their shoestrings were called shoelaces.

At school, our drawing class was on the subject of Halloween. We drew or made cutouts about pumpkins and corn shocks. One girl who could draw really well made a picture of a black cat, all hunched up and angry. I made a poster with some pumpkins in a field. In the sky above, I pasted a black cutout of an old witch with a pointed hat and flying on a broom. Our posters were hung with thumbtacks along the top of the blackboard.

Helen asked several boys to bring some pumpkins to school. With her guidance, the big girls carved out three pumpkin heads, making smiling mouths and big round eyes. She set them in a row on a shelf right above the blackboard.

My poster was right below the one in the center. After a few days, the pumpkin above my poster began to ooze from the cuts on its face. It dripped right on the old witch's pointed hat and face and made the witch look like she had some kind of beard.

I pasted my poster on page two of my scrapbook. On the poster I wrote, "It was a very angry pumpkin that spit all over the old witch." I didn't mind what the pumpkin had done since it made my poster seem alive.

This was the first year none of my brothers or sisters were in school with me. Helen was my teacher, but that was different. We didn't talk together about school. At home I was her little brother, but at school she was my teacher.

Around home, Esther and I would often talk about school, but we never talked about one thing that happened. We tried to forget it. It was a playground event of several years earlier, when Miss Young was our teacher.

One summer while school was out, the trustees built brand new boys' and girls' outhouses, to replace the old rickety ones. They were really special. Each one was surrounded by a privacy wall made of broad planks. One could only see the roof of the privy above the wall. The private courtyard was entered from the side, and the wall kept the privy door from view.

Esther and the older pupils were studying about George Washington and the Revolutionary War. Thinking about the armies and their actions, she cooked up the idea that we ought to play a game about armies on the school ground. So she called together six of the big girls and six of the big boys and said we would organize two armies. One army would be the girls, and the other would be the boys. She would be the captain of the girls, and I would command the boys.

They all thought it would be fun. The boys knew they were the best, and the girls thought they were smarter than the boys. The separate privies would be our respective forts and headquarters. A certain space around each fort would be our country.

All went well for several days. We carried out limited sorties in the open country, always respecting each other's territory. Then one day while Esther and I were home for lunch, something happened.

The boys, under the leadership of the next in command, began an attack on the girls. Just as Esther and I hurried back from lunch, we heard a lot of noise. The girls had retreated into their fort, and the boys had them surrounded. They were pelting the privy with stones and shouting, "Surrender! Surrender!"

The girls were inside, shrieking and bawling.

Just then, Miss Young came running down and pulled the boys off. She demanded to know what was going on. The girls came out sobbing their woeful tale about the mean, ugly boys. Esther and I stood at a distance, hearing each side giving their story.

Miss Young gave us all the most severe scolding I had ever heard. She also blamed Esther and me for dreaming up such an awful game: "Any more of this, and I'll have to tell your parents."

The war was over. Both sides had lost, but Esther and I had lost the most. We never said one word about it ever again, at home or at school.

Sometimes when I was alone, I thought about that episode. I was embarrassed that we had led others into the war game and helped to set up a scene that got out of hand. As I gradually got over it, I thought about a verse of song we sang at school:

Never sigh for what is past,
For the future do not pine;
Though the day not long will last,
Every hour it has is thine.

Fill it then with duty done,
With a purpose strong and true,
Night will have a victory won
That belongs to you.

Now these several years later, why did I have to think of it again? I would soon be twelve years old, and things people said and did would start me thinking about growing up. I wasn't a little boy any more, and I wouldn't be a teenager for another year. I didn't quite fit in anywhere. Having Helen as my teacher was good for me. She helped me feel comfortable just as I was.

I just knew this was going to be a good year.

10

Worries

One Saturday afternoon I went down to my little house in the woods. I hadn't been there for awhile and thought it might need some repair. My sylvan home was a little damp and lonesome looking but otherwise all right.

Since it was a nice day, I fooled around there for some time. I was thinking about a man the family was talking about, who had stayed awake all night worrying. Finally they had to take him to a special hospital for treatment. He eventually got over it and was home again. I also thought a lot about many things, but I didn't stay awake at night.

Sitting there on the old stool, I decided to try something I had read about in a story. A girl planned that when she worried about something bad, she would write it in her notebook. Then she would mark over it with her pen and below it write in something good to think about. It was like making a resolution.

I took my old notebook to try something like it for myself, but it was all soaked and moldy. Instead of trying to use the wet paper, I went to the stream and got a handful of soft blue clay. There, on my "desk," I fashioned a round patty like a pancake. I smoothed it carefully and tried to write some words on it with an old pencil stub.

It didn't work. The clay was too crumbly. So I decided to make a resolution and scratch a figure on the clay as a sign. I promised myself, "I resolve to always be nice to others and never be mean at school." To record my resolve, I scratched two parallel lines across the clay pancake.

The clay would harden and preserve the lines. I wanted my resolution to become just as firm as the clay. Esther was always reminding me not to be "wishy-washy." She said I was too "flighty" and ought to be more steady.

What got me thinking was an interesting story a visiting preacher had told last summer. He was from the West, where cowboys rode bucking broncos. "To ride a horse safely and successfully," he said, "the rider must not try to sit too tightly in the saddle. Keep your feet in the stirrups and sit loose."

He drew a lesson from the story. "We should not attach ourselves too tightly to the good things God gives us. Doing so might cause us to slip and fall into trouble." As he developed the theme, he would often pause and repeat, "Sit loose!"

As I scratched the two lines in the clay, I told myself, "Sit loose!"

Eva was becoming more interested in Reuben Carper. She didn't say much about it. But when she was home on weekends, she played some of the love songs on the Victrola. We knew that he visited his brother's family where she was boarding. According to local custom, for him to be actually dating her, he would need to visit her here at our home.

At this time I happened to be reading a book Helen had given me, *The Little Shepherd of Kingdom Come*. Set during the Civil War, it was about Chadwick Beauford and a neighbor named Melissa, who had fallen in love. They were from the South, but chance had separated them. He became an officer in the Union army, but she remained faithful to the South.

Finally it all worked out for Chad and Melissa. The war was over, and he returned home. All was forgiven as they sat talking together on the veranda of his childhood house, now his.

Finally, as if by mutual thought, they rose together and stood there close to each other, looking at the starry sky. Then, standing on her tiptoes, Melissa softly kissed the saber scar on Chad's cheek. Looking into her lovely eyes, he gently kissed her tender lips and whispered, "Will you be my wife?"

For me, the word *wife* took away all the romance. A wife was someone working around the house and garden, not a romantic young maiden. I wished he had said instead, "Will you marry me?" Then the moonlight and romance would have floated on into a lovely future.

Back in school, we were reading about Benjamin Franklin and other strong men of early America. They had worked hard. One of the poems we learned was about work and success. I put it in my scrapbook.

This is the Gospel of Labor,
Ring it, ye bells of the kirk!
    The Lord of Love
    Came down from above,
To live with the men who work.

This is the rose he planted,
Here in this thorn-cursed soil;
    While Heaven is blessed
    With perfect rest,
The blessing of earth is toil.
    —Henry van Dyke

Toil was all right to make one strong. I didn't mind reading about it. And yet, I always envied the dog lying there, doing nothing when I was cleaning out the dirty stables.

11

Fatal Damage

Franklin was interested in many different things. His latest interest was about handwriting. He had obtained a little book that explained how handwriting revealed the disposition and character of the writer. It had illustrations of certain words or lines written by great men and women. There were also examples from unsuccessful characters.

As expected, we tried to see how we scored with our own handwriting. With his clear and simple penmanship, Franklin came out well. Esther claimed a good chance of success with the vertical, open style she had learned down south in Amelia, Virginia.

After examining my handwriting, Esther concluded, "Your penmanship lacks purpose."

Franklin was easier on me. He reminded Esther, "Levi still has time to develop a good style." Esther was always trying to analyze me.

We were all home for Thanksgiving and had a

wonderful time. Mama and Helen worked together making dinner. They introduced several new things we had never tasted before. I thought they were really good.

Dad even liked them, or at least he said so. He didn't go for strange or unusual salads or desserts. For Dad, it was simple things, nothing fancy—just salt and no pepper. Once when a special meat dish with herbs and spices was served, Dad shoved certain unfamiliar bits to the side of his plate. When Mama asked him about it, he said, "That's my doubtful pile."

Thanksgiving had been fun, and Christmas was even more enjoyable. Eva brought us a new Victrola record of Christmas songs. She also brought along something special. It was a large box of Shrafts special chocolate candy, but it wasn't for us. Reuben had given it to her for Christmas! We weren't offered any, and she didn't even let us look in the box.

Eva always called him Reuben, but we called him Rube. We began to talk about "Eva and Rube." A friendship was developing between them.

I know I will never forget the Christmas that followed. Franklin gave me a nice big Erector set and a toy steam engine. I began working on a project at once. I would mount the little engine on a four-wheel truck made from the Erector pieces.

My plan was going well. The truck was assembled, and I was figuring out how to mount the engine. It had to be just right so the belt would line up with the pulleys and wheels. I was pushing it around on the floor to see how it would work when Dad reminded me it was time to gather the eggs. I placed it carefully on the sewing machine, out of reach of little Junie (Henry Jr.) and went for the eggs.

It usually took at least a half-hour to hunt the eggs. By hurrying, I cut the time a little. My project was foremost on my mind. After putting the egg basket in the basement, I hurried up the steps to get back to my truck project.

I arrived just in time to see Junie on tiptoes, pushing at my engine contraption. I was too late to stop

him. It rolled off and hit the floor with a thud. The result was devastating. The engine received a big dent in the boiler, right where the glass water gauge was located. The damage was fatal. Repair was not possible. Steam pressure would always push out any plugs we tried to install.

"You shouldn't be mad at Junie," Mama said. "He didn't do it on purpose. He just wanted to play with it."

Now the shiny new engine was useless. I cried awhile, and little Junie went to play in another room. I took the now-useless Erector truck apart and began to plan another project, maybe some kind of an engine.

These days, I began to think more about Eva and Rube. One Saturday she had taken us to meet the Jake Carper family and to see the Sun Hill schoolhouse, where she was teaching. She introduced us to the family. After talking awhile, we drove a short distance to the school.

Sun Hill was just about like Webster except that it didn't have any hills for sledding. Meeting the Carpers and seeing Eva's school made me wonder more and more about what Eva would finally be doing. She was special to me, and I didn't like the thought of her leaving the family.

Back in school after Christmas, we again began our usual snowball games and sledding. In our readers, we saw stories about the pioneer days, with log cabins and wild animals. In one of our history lessons, Helen gave us a little poem to learn. It was to show us that in spite of sad things, there was always hope.

A shipwrecked sailor buried on this coast
Bids thee take sail,
Full many a bark when we were lost,
Braved the gale.

I printed it in my scrapbook. Below it, I drew a picture of a beach with a little tombstone. I scratched some make-believe words on it for the epitaph. I had just learned the word *epitaph*. It expressed some appreciation for the departed and was written on their tombstones. Helen had read to us the first lines of an epitaph written by Robert Louis Stevenson:

Under the wide and starry sky
Dig the grave and let me lie.

She read us some poems from his *Child's Garden of Verses.* I liked the one that began—

Dark brown is the river,
Golden is the sand.
It flows along forever,
With trees on either hand.

I liked poetry. Sometime I was going to try writing poems.

Rube and the Family

12

Eva's Date

Next week would come Valentine's Day again. As usual, we would be making valentines in our drawing class. There wouldn't be as many to pass around this year because a lot of the big boys and girls had finished school last year.

This year I was going to try real hard to make neat valentines so people wouldn't be ashamed to show them around. Last year I had received one that I just stuck down in my desk. I pitied the little girl who gave it to me, and I was too timid to thank her for it and to tell her I thought it was pretty.

This year I was going to give a valentine to Lillie Eitnier and maybe to Ruth Bomberger. We boys didn't usually give valentines to each other. There were two girls at Webster who also went to my church. I wasn't going to give them any. I was afraid they wouldn't like it and might tease me. It was always hard for me to know how to act around girls.

One day at home, a huge secret was revealed. Eva told Mama that Reuben was coming to visit her on Sunday afternoon. I was anxious to see what he really looked like. So far I had only seen a snapshot of him. In the picture, he looked tall and seemed to have a rather large nose. Of course, big men usually had large features.

I didn't know how boys and girls dated. People just said, "So and so are dating." Maybe the boy just went to visit the girl with her family, or perhaps they just sat around together by themselves. I decided to prepare for Rube's visit in a way that wouldn't embarrass Eva. So on that Sunday, after my noontime chicken chores were done, I made my plans.

I changed into my school clothes and got into my Sunday shoes. After I made sure my face was clean and my hair combed, I sneaked into the parlor. I selected a chair where I was going to sit. That left two soft chairs and the sofa for Eva and Rube to choose for their seats. I took a book and planned how I would sit as though I were concentrating on its contents.

All this took place while Eva was out in the other part of the house, talking to Helen and Esther. She sounded nervous. One thing bothered me: we had two front doors, one for the parlor, and the other for the front room, the regular part of the house. How would Rube know on which to knock?

When at last Rube rolled up in his Buick, Eva came by a side door into the parlor. She didn't notice me quietly sitting on my chair. Rube knocked at the parlor door, and she opened it. They each said hello and turned to enter.

Then she saw me sitting there. She made some motions to me that I ignored and just sat there quietly "reading." They sat down on the soft chairs, not on the sofa, and began small talk about things like the weather.

After awhile I looked up and saw Esther at the side door, making frantic motions and trying to mouth some words. I got the message. I was supposed to leave the room.

So I got up nonchalantly and strolled out to the kitchen, where Esther gave me a lecture of medium intensity for being so dumb. It was now clear to me that Rube was not visiting the family and especially not me.

I now had learned three things or perhaps just observed them. First, Eva had previously told Rube which door opened to the parlor. Next, Eva and Rube did not sit on the sofa. Last, a date did not include the family.

I pondered these discoveries as I kept analyzing the elements of a date. Thus far, I could detect no romance in their relationship like the romance I always sensed in the stories I read.

Maybe it would get better as time went on. There might be times of sweet music, lovely moonlit nights, bowers of roses, and singing birds. I tried to imagine Eva and Rube in such a setting. But we had no roses, and no nightingales to sing the sweet songs of romance. We did have whippoorwills. They could add romance, but then the hoot owls and screech owls could spoil it all.

Maybe Rube's Buick could add some romance. After all, we had only a little Overland Black Bird, about half the size of the Buick. Before going to school in the morning, I asked Mama if Eva and Rube would be dating now. She gave the usual answer, "Only time will tell."

Helen seemed more romantic than Eva. She was not timid about discussing love stories, and she often sang or hummed love songs. She made everyone seem special in a gentle sort of way. Eva was nice too. She had a way of making us all know she appreciated us. When I needed comfort, my first pick was Helen. But if I needed courage, I would look for Eva. I liked them both very, very much.

The school songs we sang were now about springtime. Helen also read to us poems about birds and flowers and other spring things. Birds were beginning to appear in bushes, making plans for nesting. One of the songs we sang was this:

Windy March is blowing
With all its might;
Brooks are overflowing
With foam all white.

Another song I liked:

Bloom, sweet violets
Warm spring winds perfuming.
All the skies are spotless blue;
All the earth is green and new.
Bloom, sweet violets,
Warm spring winds perfuming.

I wrote in my scrapbook one of the poems we had learned:

These are the things I prize
And hold of dearest worth:
Light of the sapphire skies,
Peace of the silent hills,
Shelter of forests, comfort of grass,
Singing of birds, and murmur of little rills.

I was determined now that I was going to write a poem soon. It would be about springtime, birds, streams, and maybe clouds. It wouldn't be like "In the Gloaming," full of sorrow. And it wouldn't be long either, because I didn't like to write that much.

13

Poetry

Shortly after Eva's date, when Franklin and I were talking together, I asked him why Mama had said "Only time will tell."

"She probably meant she didn't know," Franklin said, "or maybe she just didn't want to talk about it. But I have an idea of my own. A few boys living near Sun Hill said they know Rube and Eva have been seeing each other for some time, ever since he returned from the West."

Franklin added, "I think the reason they had their date at our home was probably to make their growing friendship a part of the family. I don't know Rube very well. My first impression of him might improve when I get to know him better."

Spring was a time of muddy roads and soft fields. We started early, planting and transplanting seeds in flats. After the seedlings were big enough, the flats would be shifted out to the cold frames, where the plants would harden for several weeks before being planted out in the fields.

We also cut seed potatoes for planting. Each piece was supposed to have two or three eyes for sprouting. The pieces were dusted to keep them from spoiling, then stored in the basement till planting time.

There were still two months before school would be out. Our recess games were prisoners' base and parlay over. Conversation among the boys was often about automobiles—how much they cost, and how fast they could go.

One boy said his uncle had a Buick that could go over sixty miles an hour. I wondered whether Rube's could go that fast. Dad never drove our car over forty miles an hour. It was several years since Weidmans had changed from a horse and buggy to a Model T Ford.

We continued to learn poems. Now Helen was teaching us one about rain, by a poet named Robert Loveman. I copied the first two verses in my scrapbook:

It isn't raining rain to me,
It's raining daffodils;
In every dimpled drop I see
Wild flowers on the hills.

The clouds of gray engulf the day
And overwhelm the town;
It isn't raining rain to me,
It's raining roses down.

I was ready to work on my own poem. Spring

was in the air, so it was the right time. I had been practicing on rhyming couplets. Helen told me to get the feel of rhythm. The lines should have the same number of syllables, and the last words should rhyme. Of course, I already knew that. What I need-ed most was an idea, something interesting and romantic.

I wrote several practice couplets. Helen said the best poems were usually about familiar subjects. Following her advice, I composed a few lines:

The wind is blowing against the screen,
I wished it wouldn't be so mean.

There was another couplet about some apple blossom petals I saw in an old bucket:

A petal, a petal,
It's in the kettle.

I decided to write my first poem about my favorite little stream that ran by my house in the woods:

The Stream
Pretty little crystal stream,
You have such a merry gleam;
As you pass through many a crook
And through many a shady nook.
And you tell a pretty story,
Of the apple blossoms hoary;
Of the busy honey bees,
Getting honey from the trees.

I thought it compared well with Robert Louis Stevenson's poems. Maybe I could become a poet. I showed it to Helen to see what she thought. She said it was really nice. Now I was ready to see what Esther would say about it when she came home on the weekend.

So at a suitable time, after she had finished telling about her week at Lititz High, I showed her my poem "The Stream." After reading it, she didn't say it was either good or bad. She simply used it to demonstrate her newly acquired knowledge of the English language, especially as it applied to poetry. She used big words like *metaphor* and *simile*.

"*Gleam* is not a good word to describe a stream," she said. "Streams don't gleam; they sparkle."

"Well," I said, "*sparkle* doesn't rhyme."

"That's the point. You're forcing a rhyme by using a poor word choice. That violates one of the rules for good poetry."

Esther also pointed out a few other things: "*Hoary* is used to describe an old man's hair and not spring blossoms. And furthermore, bees don't get honey from trees. They sip nectar from flowers and blossoms on trees, then make it into honey."

What she had said to me about my poetry didn't make me mad. But of course, it didn't make me feel really good, either. Somehow, it made me change my attitude toward her. Esther seemed more grown-up. I thought about the things she had pointed out to me and decided they were all true.

I put the poem back in my dresser drawer. I didn't write it in my scrapbook because it was not a part of my schoolwork. But the real reason was that I knew it wasn't good enough. Another thing I noticed about Esther's exchange on the poem was that she hadn't made fun of me. She had treated me like a real person.

14

Changes

At the supper table a few days after Rube's visit, Mama said, "Well, I guess we can't keep it a secret any longer: Eva is engaged to Reuben. They are planning to get married sometime this summer."

The news came as a shock to me. I had thought of such an event as being way out ahead, far in the future, not anytime so soon. I had always thought of Eva as an older sister and a schoolteacher. She had always been with us and belonged to us. Now all that would be changing. She would be going somewhere else, away from home.

Helen didn't seem to be surprised. In fact, she smiled when Mama made the announcement. Eva had probably talked about it to her before. Mama must have known it too, back when she said, "Only time will tell."

Franklin hadn't thought too much about the marriage prospect before, and Betty and Junie were too little to be in the upper levels of serious family matters. However, it did bother Esther. She thought she should have been included in the secret matters of her sisters from the beginning.

Now we began to see more of Rube. Sometimes he would bring Eva home from school on Friday evenings, returning again on Sunday afternoons to take her back to Jake Carper's. Eva's coming wedding also became an important part of our conversation and conjectures.

Dad never talked much about such things, and Mama's remarks were only about weddings in general. She said the plans for the wedding were up to Eva. It was her project.

Eva did talk to Helen about the wedding. Sometimes I could hear them up in their room, talking. Once I heard them in the parlor, talking about wedding dresses and how things had been done at certain weddings where they had been guests.

Weddings usually took place in the bride's home, with the district bishop performing the ceremony. A wedding dinner followed. There were many things to plan: guests to invite and selecting certain persons to be attendants. Those things didn't interest me, so I paid little attention to the conversation.

Franklin and I did wonder where Rube and Eva would live. They would probably have to buy a house somewhere or maybe a farm like his brother had. Sometimes, when the youngest child was a son, he would take over the family farm, and the family would retire to a house in town.

Franklin and I finally arrived at a conclusion. Maybe Rube and Eva would live in Lititz with his mother and two older sisters. They had plenty of room, and that's where Rube was living now. That also was not too far from his place of work, the Hershey & Leaman Lumber Company, down near the railroad.

Maybe Eva would keep on teaching. We knew of several young wives who had jobs in the local silk mill. We never told our ideas to the others. That wouldn't have been wise.

Finally school was over. The wedding date had been set for the last week in June. Helen was busy helping Eva sew her different wedding dresses. Because wedding dinners were something special, Mama engaged Mrs. Long, a consultant, to help with the table setting and the menu.

The usual potatoes and gravy would not be good enough. A proper meal would be served. *Menu* was a new word to me. Eva said, "It's a list of foods at a meal, such as at a restaurant." Since I had never eaten at a restaurant, I still didn't know exactly what *menu* meant.

One evening as we were sitting together talking, Eva told us about the wedding trip they were planning. They would probably go to a place called Watkins Glen in New York and return by way of the beach at Atlantic City, New Jersey.

"I bought a bathing suit at Watt & Shands in Lancaster," Eva said.

"Show it to us," Helen suggested.

"It's too personal," Eva replied.

After Helen urged her some more, Eva got it and held it up for us to see how it would fit. It was dark blue and had a little frill instead of a collar. The sleeves went almost to the wrists, and the pant legs reached down below the knees. It had an extra skirt that went from the waist to just above the knees.

Mama was embarrassed and said, "Oh, Eva, put it away!"

"Where will you stay overnights while you're on your trip?" I asked Eva.

She explained about hotels. "You drive up to the door, and a man will show you where to park. Then a bellboy comes and carries your suitcases up to your room. He opens the door and sets your bags on the floor inside. Then he holds out his hand, and you are supposed to give him a tip."

"How much are they supposed to give?" I wondered.

"Oh, about fifty cents. I bet you would carry my things for nothing."

From what she said and how she said it, I got the idea that maybe they would take me along on their wedding trip—if I was real nice.

I didn't say anything to anyone about what I thought, but I started to be real nice to Eva. I imagined myself staying in hotels and eating "menus."

I did have a good red swimming suit. It was a boy's suit and not like Eva's. When no one was around, I looked in the Sears & Roebuck catalog at the section for women's bathing suits. They had suits for sale just like the one Eva had.

To make sure I would be really nice to Eva, I went down to my little house in the woods, where I had made my last resolution to be good. The old resolution bit of blue clay was gone. Time and a leaking roof had erased it. Repeating what I had done

before, I got a handful of the blue clay, made my resolution patty, and told myself, "I resolve to be real
nice to Eva." Again, I drew two parallel lines and left
it to harden.

School was over, so I took my scrapbook and
other odds and ends up to my room. Before putting
my scrapbook in the dresser drawer, I leafed
through it again. The poems and drawings reminded me of my happy school year just past. Helen
would not be teaching at Webster again. She was
going to be teaching down at Farmersville, far away.

Next year would be different. Eva and Helen
would both be gone. It gave me a lonesome feeling.
The chorus of a song we used to sing at school came
to my mind:

Oh, the happy, happy days gone by,
We again no more shall see.
Let them pass for days that lie ahead,
Better days shall be.

15

The Wedding

When Mama had "let the cat out of the bag" about Eva's engagement, we began trying to guess what she might be getting for an engagement present. Young men usually gave their girlfriends a special gift when they became engaged. It was supposed to be something useful that would suggest his enduring love for her.

The girls suggested various possibilities, but finally with Mama's participation, they decided it would likely be a cedar chest. And that is what it turned out to be. Rube brought it in his car. He had removed the rear cushion, allowing just enough space for it.

Rube told Eva, "Come out and see it." Eva was going to help him bring it in, but he said, "I loaded it myself, and I can bring it in myself." But after Rube coaxed it out of the car, he let her help him carry it in.

I think Mama knew in advance about the chest. After all, Eva never had a hope chest like most girls did. She was always busy going to college and teaching. Someone must have told Rube that Eva didn't have a hope chest. I suspect that Mama tipped him off.

Now the big event, Eva's wedding, was at hand. From all the talking, I knew it would be somewhat unusual. To begin with, it would take place at nine o'clock in the morning and be followed by a wedding breakfast. Not many people were invited because our house could not hold a big crowd. But it would be special because Mrs. Long, "the specialist," had done most of the planning.

Eva and a number of girls, including Helen, were dressed in white. Several of the young men wore dark suits with white shirts and black bow ties. At a certain moment, Eva and Rube would step forward and stand together at a set spot. Several of the girls dressed in white would stand beside Eva, and several of the black-tie men would stand beside Reuben.

The small audience would sit facing them, watching from their neatly arranged folding chairs borrowed from the church. Lack of space would make it necessary for the little ones to sit in another room.

Now, just before the ceremony, Rube locked his car in our garage to keep the boys from hanging on tin cans and writing JUST MARRIED all over the sides. I offered to go along and make sure the doors were all secured.

Instead of acting as entrusted, however, I made sure one of the doors wasn't locked. Why? By this time I had finally become aware that my dream of being a helper on their wedding trip had been nothing but a stupid fancy.

The ceremony began with Bishop Noah Landis giving counsel and admonitions. Then Eva and Reuben answered questions by saying "I do" at the proper places. Since the ceremony was not in a church full of people, the bishop's remarks were not extended. Then a selected group of young people sang a special hymn, and the bishop ended the service with a short benediction.

After a short period for congratulations and friendly conversation, it was time for the breakfast. This was not a time for ham and eggs, as with an ordinary breakfast. There were two tables in two adjoining rooms. As the guests gathered at the tables, they looked perplexed. There before them were tables with no food or plates.

At each place they saw neatly arranged silverware and a folded napkin. Also at each place was a sherbet glass containing mixed, diced fruit. The main table had place cards for the guests, while the other table allowed random seating. Eventually all were seated, with the bride and groom at the head of the main table, and the bishop led in a short blessing.

Some of the guests pushed their sherbets aside, assuming they were dessert. Others paused, sipping a bit from their glasses of lemonade. Finally, after watching others, all began eating their fruit sherbet. Then two young men—wearing white shirts, black bow ties, and tidy white aprons—came with trays and gathered the empty glasses. They soon returned with their trays, bringing for each guest a plate with the main course.

I didn't know what everything was called. Afterward Helen told me that each plate had a sweet potato croquet, a meat patty, and a serving of succotash. The two waiters were my own brother, Franklin, and one of the Hershey boys.

When the meal was finished, waiters took the wedding cake from the center of the table and set it before the bride and groom. A waiter brought a suitable knife and placed it beside the cake. Then the groom picked up the knife and, with the bride placing her hand on his, they cut the first piece.

Someone said, "Hey, that's the first work you did together as man and wife."

With a voice like a preacher, another person said, "And may it be ever thus."

Then the waiters distributed smaller pieces of cake to everyone.

While people were still talking, a few of us boys sneaked out to the shed to give the Buick a traditional treatment. We dangled some old paint buckets from the rear bumper and wrote JUST MARRIED all over the car with soft, blue chalk.

To top it off, I wrote on the Buick in big letters, RUBE'S BUSS. As a final stupid act, I dumped a peck of potatoes on the back seat and said, "Now, if they get hungry, they can eat potatoes."

At noon, when everything was over, Eva and Rube walked out together to get in their car and start on their honeymoon trip. We stood at a distance to watch. Their friends stood close by to see them off. As the car came backing out, we could see Rube was mad and Eva looked distressed. They took off up the hill with Rube not looking back, but Eva tried to hide her distress by waving a cheerful good-bye.

At the top of the hill, they paused. Rube cut off the tin cans and tried to erase some of the chalk. Then he climbed back in, and they drove off.

Right then I began to feel really bad for what I had done. Why had I been so mean to Eva?

16

The Serenade and Shower

After being gone about a week, the honeymooners returned. They stayed at our house several days before returning to his mother's house in Lititz, where Rube had been living. They would be living there while plans were being completed for them to move onto the farm they were buying up north, near Brickerville. Dad had worked out something to make it possible for them to buy it.

On the first night after their return, I was awakened by a lot of noise out in the front yard. I heard whistles and bells and a deep, groaning sound. The groans seemed to make the front door rattle.

Franklin awoke too, and it didn't take him long to figure what all the noise was about. "Hey! Some guys are out there serenading the newlyweds." We knew that young fellows did that sometimes. It wasn't regarded as something really bad, but just a chance to give a loud welcome and to expect a little cash handout in return.

Rube must have been expecting something. Finally he went to the front door, still dressed in his suit. He had a little trouble with the door, but it soon came open, and he shouted above the din, "Hi, you guys—a little less noise, please."

In the dark I was watching from the next room. He reached into his pocket and handed them some paper money. Then with loud thank-yous, they loaded up their cars and left. At that, I returned to our bedroom and asked Franklin, "What was that groaning noise?"

"It is made with a rosin box," he said. "A rosin box is a contraption made of wood covered with rosin in such a way that drawing one piece of wood across another, like a violin bow, makes a hideous noise."

Sometimes, to make the front door rattle, the serenaders would stretch a wire from the box to the doorknob. I guess that's why it had been hard for Rube to open the door.

After all that excitement, I finally went back to sleep.

While Eva and Rube had been away on their trip, Dad had told us a bit about how and why they were going to live on a farm. Eva had arranged for Dad to sit down with them, so they could ask his advice about their future plans.

Rube had said that the man who owned Hershey & Leaman Lumber, where he worked, wanted to sell out. He had given Rube and the other man working there an opportunity to buy him out. Dad calculated that too much money was involved, so he had advised them to try to buy a farm. He had offered to help them.

They had driven around and found a small farm for sale near Brickerville. It had fitted their needs and their purse, so he had helped them buy it. He said, "I gave them a little put-up money and endorsed their paper." I didn't understand what "paper" meant, but I guess Dad did.

Shortly after the serenade, while they were still living in Lititz, some of Helen's girlfriends arranged for a shower to be held at our house for Eva. It was a pleasant, relaxed occasion. The tension that had surrounded the events of the wedding and serenade were all gone.

The shower took place on the front lawn and porch on a weekday evening. Guests gathered around on the lawn and were talking of recent events. Some walked around, while others sat in groups on the lawn chairs. Colorful Japanese lanterns hung from the lower branches of the sour cherry trees.

On the porch were two tables. One was filled with cookies and lemonade. The other one stood ready to receive shower gifts. A men's quartet sang familiar songs, and occasionally some of the guests joined in. Then Eva opened each gift, thanking the one who gave it.

Finally, among words of well-wishing and congratulations, the guests began to leave. Eva and Reuben left with their gifts, driving back to Lititz.

When the people moved from the farm Eva and Reuben were buying, we all drove up to look it over.

Some rode along with Eva and Reuben, while the rest of us followed in our car.

The country roads wound among fields of growing corn and tobacco. Finally we turned left and drove up a hill to the farm. We jumped out to look things over. The men looked around the barn and sheds, commenting on the satisfactory condition of the buildings. The women were more interested in the house and garden.

Later we all were together on the porch, conversing about the beautiful day and making other small talk. Rube went to the little pump house at the end of the porch and tried the pump. The pump house was actually an extension of the porch. He gave the large iron handle a few pumps, and water came running out into the trough. "The pump works real well," he commented.

The women were grouped around Eva as she looked out over the road toward the valley below. She grew poetic and quoted a line about "a house upon a windy hill." She said, "That just might be a good name for our house." Then she recited a verse from a poem we knew at home:

Let me live in a house by the side of the road
Where the race of men go by—
The men who are good and the men who are bad,
As good and as bad as I.
I would not sit in the scorner's seat
Or hurl the cynic's ban—
Let me live in a house by the side of the road
And be a friend to man.
     —Sam Walter Foss

Eva said, "We just might name our farm the House by the Side of the Road."

Rube wasn't thinking about poetry. He saw other things as he looked across the road. There would be work to do and bills to pay.

I thought of a poem he could have quoted if he were the poetic type, lines I had learned at school:

This is the Gospel of Labor,
Ring it, ye bells of the kirk!
　　　　—Henry van Dyke

17

Why Did I Do It?

All the paperwork was finished, making Reuben and Eva Carper the owners of the farm. Yet it would be several weeks before they would move there. During that time, one Sunday after church, we decided to drive by the farm, just to take a passing look at it.

As we approached it, we saw some people in the orchard, picking apples. It seemed rather odd because the apples weren't ripe yet and it was Sunday. So instead of driving by, we stopped to see what was going on.

The people picking apples were the man and woman who had sold the place to the Carpers. When Dad got out of the car, they tried to act natural, as if nothing was wrong. The man said, "Why, hello Henry."

When Dad didn't reply, the man went on, giving an excuse for what they were doing: "Well, the apples would be mostly ours. They were growing when we still owned the place. Do you want some of them?"

"No," said Dad. "We would let ours get ripe."

Dad got back in the car, and we drove on. As we left, the man began loading the baskets of green apples into their car. Dad remarked, "I guess they thought we would be in church and not notice the missing apples."

"Was what he said about owning part of the apples true?" I asked.

"Often in such a case like this," Dad replied, "it's normal for the new owner to offer some of the apples to the previous owner. They usually share them on a friendly basis after they're ripe."

Shortly after that, the Carpers moved in. Now we were calling them "the Carpers" when speaking with other people. We didn't need to help much with the moving. They had things well organized and were soon settled in and established.

Eva and Rube had enough furniture for the house, plus two horses and one cow in the barn. During the summer they had been buying some necessary farm machinery at farm sales.

Now things returned to normal at home. Franklin and I went back to our schedule of work and play. He was seventeen years old and had money of his own to spend. He used some of it to buy a nice fishing rod and reel and a tackle box. For me, he bought a short bamboo pole and some fishing tackle.

In the evening after work, we often went fishing at Zartman's dam. When we caught real nice fish, we brought them home in a bucket of water and dumped them in our spring. We wanted to start a school of fish there like the one we saw in Lititz Springs, at the park. But the only ones we ever saw were the ones we put there.

Occasionally, before going to sleep at night, we talked together about personal things. It was easier to talk that way in the dark, away from everyone else. Franklin read a lot of books and often studied his Bible. I liked to talk to him and ask him about things I didn't understand. He always answered me and never teased me about things that bothered me.

One time I asked him, "Why do people sometimes do things that turn out to be real bad, especially when they should know better?"

"Well," he said, "some people have a mean streak inside that gets the best of them." I didn't ask him to explain what that meant. But I wondered whether maybe I had a mean streak.

I wondered about some of the mean things I had done. Why did I spoil Eva's honeymoon by messing up Rube's Buick? The faint chalk marks could still be seen on its side where I had written, *RUBE'S BUSS*. It would always be there; they couldn't wash it off.

Two other things I had done still bothered me. When I was a little six-year-old, still living back at Eshleman's farm, I robbed some little ground sparrows' nests. Walking along the meadow stream one nice summer day, I began looking for ground sparrow nests in the stream bank. Whenever I found one, I would snatch at and throw it away, eggs and all. I did it to three nests.

When Eva found out about it, she scolded me for being so mean and added, "I thought you liked birds!"

I cried and just said, "I don't know why I did that."

I was involved in another mean thing two years later at Possum Hollow, when Franklin was building those nice little wren houses. Another eight-year-old boy was visiting at our house with his parents. He was going with me along the road. We each had a big stick and were having a good time knocking off the tops of weeds.

When we came to the lawn, I entered through the gate. I still wasn't done knocking things down. Then I saw two wren boxes hanging on the cherry trees. I laughed and began busting up the boxes with my stick. The other boy helped, and the boxes were soon in splinters.

Just then Dad and Franklin saw what I was doing. Dad took my arm and, pulling me aside, gave me a talking to I never forgot. What still bothered me most was seeing Franklin crying as he picked up the pieces. I still could not imagine why I had done such a thing.

Lying there in bed, with my mind still mulling over mean streaks, I asked Franklin one more question. "What should people do who have a mean streak?"

He replied, "It would help if they would think twice before doing something dumb."

I had an idea that Franklin probably knew I was asking those questions with myself in mind. I was afraid it was going to take more to get rid of my mean streak than going down to my little house and scratching some marks on a patty of clay.

In the morning, when I got out of bed, I felt a little better. From now on, I was going to think twice before doing something mean. Maybe I would have to think three times. My mean streak might need extra work.

18

The Fight Corner

What we called the Fight Corner fascinated me ever since the first time Dad pointed it out to us on our way to Possum Hollow. There it was, like a little toy forest at the edge of our field, along the road near Phares Zartman's place. It was a three-cornered piece, not over a half-acre in size, filled with tall locust trees and small cedars. The ground was covered with honeysuckle vines climbing the tree trunks and almost hiding bits of old wooden-rail fence.

I used to imagine myself building an Indian tepee, right in the middle of it, hidden by the bushes. Crows liked to sit in the treetops. We could hear their cawing across the fields. Sometimes when we flushed up a covey of quail, they flew for shelter under the honeysuckle.

When we pushed the vines apart, we could see the remains of an old dirt roadbed. One time when we asked Dad why that bit of woods right there in our field was never farmed, he explained it to us.

"Long ago, the area was held in large tracts of land. As it began to be divided into smaller family farms, access lanes were needed to reach the properties, some of which divided different properties. Because of constant general use, many of them eventually changed from private lanes to public roads."

That was the situation right here, where the road from Lexington divided what later would become the Zartman and Shreiner farms. The road had once been part of the Shreiner land.

Because of the property lines at this point, the road had to take a really sharp turn. As time went on, the township decided to ease the sharp curve by cutting the corner. To do this, the township used some of Zartman's land and gave back a triangle of Shreiner's land (used to be part of the road).

Everyone, including the landowner, was pleased with the project. But when it was finished, trouble began between the Zartmans and Shreiners about who owed whom for the land that was used.

Both owners had logical claims. The Zartmans said they should have the old bit of abandoned roadbed in compensation for what they had given up. The Shreiners claimed, and rightfully so, that the old roadbed had been a part of their property in the original land grant.

Instead of trying to come to an agreement, they just continued to argue over it. And the land just stayed there. The old timers called it the Fight Corner, but the present generation had all but forgotten about it.

The bend in the road was still rather sharp, making it difficult for wagons or cars to pass each other there. When tall corn was growing in the field inside the bend, it was impossible for drivers of meeting vehicles to see each other far enough ahead to take evasive action.

Once Dad had an accident there, his car collided with another one at the corner. Because they weren't driving fast, there was little damage to the cars. Both men got out to look things over and seemed to agree that they probably shared the fault. The other man said in Pennsylvania Dutch, "*Mer hen allebeed pletzlich gschtoppt* (we both stopped on the spot)."

Both went on their way, and the matter was dropped. Dad had his fender straightened for eight dollars. In a couple weeks, Dad got a letter from the other man, stating his damage amounted to twenty-five dollars, and it was Dad's responsibility to pay it. Dad thought it wasn't his to pay but went ahead and paid it anyway.

That made Franklin mad. He said the man knew it was his own fault, but because Dad was easy to get along with, the other man took unfair advantage of him. It was true that Dad was easy to get along with, so the matter ended there.

One day Dad went to talk with Phares Zartman about the Fight Corner, simply calling it "the piece of land." Dad said, "Since I have the Shreiner farm now, I would like to settle the matter and pay you something for the land. As it is now, it just stands there useless."

"Well," Phares told him, "I can't sell it or take money for it because I don't hold title to it."

Dad said, "I don't own it either. The latest deed to the Shreiner farm didn't show it as his property."

To settle the matter, Dad offered to give Phares the locust trees. They would make a lot of good locust posts, much in demand. That pleased Phares.

So they both got together and sawed down the trees. They used Phares's good crosscut saw and did the work together. Then Phares asked Dad if he could borrow his *Weggeli* (little wagon) to haul the posts to his place. He often borrowed Dad's *Weggeli*. It had small iron wheels that kept it low to the ground, making it good for hauling heavy things.

This time when he borrowed it, he asked if he could keep it for a week to do a little other hauling of his own. While he had it, I happened to be walking past his place one day. He was just getting the horses around to hitch them to the wagon. In the process, old Bawly stepped on one of the singletrees and broke it in two. Old Bawly was his big friendly lead horse. I just walked on and forgot to say anything about it.

When he returned the wagon, he apologized to Dad about the single tree. "*Ach, de alt Bawly waar so dabbich* (oh, old Baldy was so clumsy)." When we checked the wagon, we saw that instead of trying to fix the old singletree, he had put on a brand new one, much better than the broken one.

After the locust trees were gone, Dad worked at the corner, pulling stumps and burning brush until it was all cleaned up. "We'll farm the corner," Dad said, "but we still don't properly own it. Someone else, sometime in the future, can settle that legal matter."

Now the Fight Corner was gone, and only pleasant memories remained. I was older now and had forgotten my childhood fantasies about Indian tepees. Sometimes now, tall corn would grow on *both* sides of the road at what had become the Friendly Corner.

From Convert to Missionary

19

Miss Eichelberger Teaches

In addition to all the work required to grow and market vegetables, Dad continued to build more chicken house space. The latest addition was a hen house in the meadow, down near the spring. It would have four pens, each large enough to hold a hundred hens.

I helped to build the hen house, doing things that didn't require carpenter skill, such as nailing down boards already tacked into place. Each pen had roost platforms and properly arranged rows of nests. Dad built stands for the water buckets and proper feed hoppers. The stands and hoppers Dad built were better than the metal ones sold in the feed stores.

Once I heard two friendly neighbor men talking about our winter butter-and-egg business. "You know what?" one of them said. "I think Henry has more money left over in the winter than in the summer."

In local conversation, "money left over" meant "profit." It was true that cash was often more plentiful in the winter. That's how Dad got enough money together to pay for farmland.

Another interesting thing Dad told us was his plan to buy a Delco electric light plant. He said we needed it to produce eggs in the winter. When the days grew shorter in the fall and winter, hens didn't lay as many eggs. The hens needed light to give them a full day to eat and drink and lay eggs.

At five o'clock each morning, the electric lights would be turned on till daylight arrived, but would not be turned on in the evening. A good healthy hen was expected to lay an egg each day during the laying season.

"I'm also going to have our house wired for lights," Dad said. That excited all of us. Now we were going to have lights just like the people in Lexington and Brunnerville. Our rooms would be so bright that we could just sit around the room in chairs to read, instead of huddling around the coal oil lamp at the table.

I certainly hated the smell of coal oil. Recently we had begun to say *kerosene* instead of *coal oil*. Eva and Helen started that change in terms, but it didn't change the smell. Now if I had an electric light close enough, maybe I could read in bed sometimes like Paul Huber said he did.

September came, and again it was time for school. Helen had packed up, and Dad had driven her down to Farmersville to teach at its one-room school. Esther began spending the school week in Lititz. Like last year, she would be staying at the Ephraim Eby home.

In January and February, Franklin planned to go to Harrisonburg, Virginia, where he was enrolling for a Six-Week Bible Term at Eastern Mennonite School (EMS). Most interesting of all, little Betty would be a beginner at Webster.

This year, Miss Eichelberger was going to be our teacher at Webster. She was a country girl from somewhere near Manheim and had earned her teacher's certificate at MSNS, as had our other teachers.

The first weeks of school were always a little mixed up. Boys fourteen years and older were allowed to begin two weeks later than the rest of us. That way they could help with more of the fall farmwork. This year, that put me in the position of "big boy" during those two weeks. I lost no time before showing off around the playground, planning the games, and making decisions.

My lofty position ended as soon as the big boys came to school from their extended vacation. Without a second thought, they took over the playground. When I tried to maintain my position in a certain situation, one boy gave me a punch with his fist. After I finally gave up trying to be one of the big boys, they let me play along, just as though I were one of them. Everything finally settled down to normal on the playground.

Things in the schoolroom weren't like last year. Miss Eichelberger didn't give us special things to do, such as making scrapbooks and learning poems. She just stuck with the basic things that were in our schoolbooks. Everyone began to relax and take things a little too easy. Sometimes she would mispronounce words, and her sentences often sounded like some of the farm ladies talk. It didn't matter. No one seemed to notice.

One evening she stopped in to visit Mama. She wanted to see if she could board and room with us. Thus far, she had been staying with the Andy Hackmans, up at the top of the hill where the Ekerts used to live. She said, "It makes me tired, walking up and down the hills to school every day."

It sounded a bit like she wasn't too pleased with staying with the old couple, either. After some thought, Mama said, "Well, you may stay with us. We have the room. Eva and Helen are away, and Esther is at Lititz all week."

So Miss Eichelberger's father came one day and helped her pack up and move out of Hackmans' house and into the girls' room in our house. After she moved in, her father would bring her every Monday morning and come back on Friday evenings to take her home.

Last year I was used to having my teacher living in our home, but that was my sister Helen. This was different. I wondered how it would be to have this unrelated teacher here, with me sitting at the same table with her for breakfast and supper. I guess Mama would have said, "Time will tell."

20

Revival Meetings

When Miss Eichelberger began staying at our house, I discovered that I could misbehave at school because she was afraid to say anything to Mama about it. For some reason, I didn't think I was being bad; I was just acting like the other big boys acted.

We didn't make fun of her or act disrespectful; we just didn't behave as well as we did last year. Miss Eichelberger seemed frustrated and impatient. We should have known better.

Early fall was usually the time churches would hold their revival meetings. They took place at various churches at different times. This year there were revival meetings at the Lititz Mennonite Church. The evangelist was a zealous little preacher from Lancaster, a gifted speaker who held the audience spellbound.

He was especially good with the stories he told that drove home the importance of being a Christian.

His illustrations effectively demonstrated the necessity of deciding to act at once, without delay. Some people made the right choice in time to receive great blessings; others, because of delay, were lost.

One story was about a young man, out West somewhere. He knew what was right or wrong and always wanted to make the vital decision to get his life straightened out. But he put it off. Then an unexpected accident occurred, and his life was "suddenly snuffed out."

The invitation hymn that followed was "Almost Persuaded." Its last verse struck to the heart of his message:

"Almost persuaded," harvest is past!
"Almost persuaded," doom comes at last!
"Almost" cannot avail, "Almost" is but to fail!
 Sad, sad, that bitter wail, "Almost" but lost!
 —P. P. Bliss

A number of young folks stood while that hymn was being sung.

As we drove home after each service, we would discuss the message, referring to stories told and mentioning names of those who responded. We knew some of them, but others were strangers from beyond our community. People came from several miles to hear the messages. The minister was well-known.

We couldn't all go to the meetings every night. One of us had to stay home to round up the chickens and coax them into the hen house before it was dark. They preferred to stay out and roost around in the fences and bushes. After they were all inside, we would be sure to close and lock all the doors.

When it was my turn to take care of the chickens, I would stay up to hear the others tell how the meeting went. I would ask about the songs and stories and how many people stood. I always asked if Paul Huber was there. He was my buddy, and we usually sat together in church. Paul was in my Sunday school class.

At church, the older folks usually sat forward. The young people about ten to twelve years old sat together in the middle. The teenagers and those slightly older but unmarried had charge of the back benches. When the invitation hymns were sung, people expected responses from the back benches, especially from those not yet members of the church.

One Tuesday evening when it was my turn to stay home, I waited up as usual to hear about the meeting. I didn't want to miss anything that went on. One of those who stood was an older person in the front benches. Then Franklin said, "Oh, yes, Paul Huber stood."

I was struck cold by the statement and wondered, *What about me?* Paul was my age, and I never thought about standing. The whole matter of revival meetings had been about other people and what they did or said. It took me a long time to go to sleep that Tuesday night.

In the morning I made up my mind to talk to Mama about it. If Paul was now going to be a member of the church and I wasn't, I would be like one of those people the preacher talked about. I would be "lost in the sea, outside the ark of safety."

When I told Mama how I felt, she said she would talk to Dad about it. All day at school, I was nervous. In the evening when I brought the basket of eggs to the basement, Dad was there with Mama. They must have planned to talk to me away from the others.

Dad said, "Children usually wait till they're in their teenage years to make a decision for Christ and the church."

I felt hurt and alone and began to cry. "Paul is my age," I said, "and he stood last night. Besides, I'll be thirteen in a few months, and it might be a long time before another series of revival meetings."

Mama said she agreed. "If you've thought so much about your own situation, you ought to go ahead and do what's in your heart."

Then Dad agreed, too, and I began to feel better.

It was Wednesday, and this was my night to stay home again. I had to take two nights in succession to care for the hens, so it would be Thursday before I could go to another meeting. Mama said that the extra day would give me a little more time to think about it. I didn't need the extra time; I knew what I wanted to do.

The next day went by slowly. In the evening when I was finished with putting the chickens in the house, I went right to bed; I was afraid to hear what the others would say about the services and what took place. I was just thinking about how it would be when I stood up in the whole church full of people on Thursday night.

21

"Come Home"

Finally, it was Thursday evening, and we were on the way to church. Conversation flowed freely as we drove along, but I didn't take my usual part. I just sat there. When we arrived, the parking lot was almost full, but we finally found a place in the back lot. As we got out of the car, we could hear the congregation singing.

We entered by the side door and found a seat near the front. I sat beside Dad because all the benches farther back were full. The ushers were placing folding chairs in the aisles.

While people gathered, we always sang hymns until it was time to begin. If people came early, we sometimes could sing three hymns. When enough people were gathered, the chorister would just stand up in front and lead his hymn selections. Some people called it "singing the people in." It was an enjoyable part of the service.

As we sat there singing, I looked up at the front benches to see how many people were sitting there. During revivals, it was the custom for those who had stood in the meetings to sit on the front benches during the remaining evenings. Now I was close enough to count them—sixteen thus far. I saw Paul Huber among them.

It was time for the meeting to start, so the chorister took his seat. Then our preacher, Jacob Hershey, rose from the preacher's bench behind the pulpit and conducted the opening. After reading a passage of Scripture and making some comments, he added his appreciation for the way the Word of God was finding a place in the hearts of the listeners.

He said, "Let us pray," and we turned and knelt at our benches. His prayers were always short and to the point. At his "Amen," we rose and sat again as before.

After the chorister led another hymn, the evangelist rose from the preacher's bench and stood behind the pulpit. His first words were to "converts" sitting on the front benches. He quoted several verses from the Bible, followed by words of blessing and encouragement. He usually finished by saying, "And it is my hope and prayer that tonight many more will make the same wise decision."

Then he began the message of the evening. He opened his Bible, held it before him, and began, "This evening I am reading to you from the prophet Isaiah, chapter fifty-three." When he finished, he closed the Bible, laid it on the pulpit, and commented on the passage.

"I call your attention to the sixth verse; that is the

text of my message to you tonight. I repeat, Isaiah fifty-three six. Repeat it after me—Isaiah fifty-three six. Now let me read what it says to us: 'All we like sheep have gone astray. We have turned every one to his own way, and the Lord has laid on him the iniquity of us all.'" He had us repeat the words with him.

Then he began his sermon. He pointed out that the verse began with "all" and ended with "all." "There are two *alls*, but they are different. The first *all* refers to the lost, while the last speaks of the saved. There are two *alls*, and it makes *all* the difference in which of the *alls* you are."

He preached a powerful message, with illustrations showing the folly of delay and the wisdom of hearing and obeying "the call." As the sermon ended, there was silence. Looking over the audience, I could see the older ladies fanning with fans the local funeral parlor had given the church.

Then the chorister announced the invitation hymn. "Hymn number 502" was all he said. I could hear the shuffle of books being taken from the racks. Dad opened our *Church and Sunday School Hymnal*, and at 502 I saw "Softly and Tenderly Jesus Is Calling." I looked at the words and decided I was going to stand when we got to "linger," in the second verse. We began to sing softly, as the chorister led while seated. The evangelist would speak words of invitation as we sang.

We began the second verse. My heart was pounding, and I was scared.

> Why should we tarry when Jesus is pleading,
> Pleading for you and for me?
> Why should we linger . . . ?   —Will L. Thompson

I stood up, but the evangelist didn't see me because I was so short. He kept looking past me to the bigger people toward the back.

Dad whispered in my ear, "Raise your arm." So I raised my arm like we did in school. He still didn't notice, so I began to wave it a little. That caught his eye.

"Why, God bless you, young man," he said. I sat down with relief. As the hymn went on, he continued his urgings: "Will there be someone else with the courage of this young man to stand right now and make the same wise choice?" The hymn ended with a plea,

> Come home . . . , come home . . .,
> Ye who are weary, come home . . .;
> Earnestly, tenderly, Jesus is calling,
> Calling, O sinner, come home!

After the benediction, I went to the front and joined the others around the front benches. The evangelist took his little book and wrote in it my name, my age, and my address. As he was writing, my mind turned to the closing words of a well-known hymn:

> Yes my name's written there,
> On the page white and fair,
> In the book of thy kingdom,
> Yes, my name's written there.

Now I would be one of
the new people in the
church. Maybe a lot of
things that bothered me would go away.

But some things would be the same. Tomorrow
was Friday. I would be back in school, and at home I
would be tending the chickens. But I knew there
would be new things coming along. I knew I could
talk to Franklin about it as we lay in bed, exchanging
thoughts and ideas.

22

Learning New Things

When we got home from church that Thursday night, I didn't stay up to talk with the others about the meeting. I was tired and didn't want to talk, because it might have involved me. I went right up to bed and was asleep before Franklin came upstairs. Then, the first thing I knew, it was morning. I had to think awhile to remember what day it was.

When I became fully awake, I knew it was Friday morning, and I remembered what had happened at church the night before. Franklin was already downstairs. For some reason, he didn't punch me awake that morning as he usually did. When I went downstairs, no one said anything about last evening's meeting. They all seemed too timid to say anything. I could understand; I didn't want to say anything either.

Fridays at school were usually when we had our drawing class. It was an easy day; we just had our usual lessons without any extra work. Sometimes our other teacher used to read to us for about fifteen minutes right after the noon recess. The day started as usual, and I was getting back into my regular routine. Then something happened at morning recess.

I saw the Snavely girls talking to some of the bigger girls. As they talked, they would glance over to where I was standing. It looked as though they might be talking about me. I had no idea what could have been of interest to them, but at noon recess I found out.

They had been to the Thursday night meeting at Lititz and were telling everybody about what I had done. I couldn't understand why it would have been of any interest to them. Even John Zartman came up, stood facing me, and gave me a pleasant and friendly smile. He didn't say anything. No one else said anything either; they just acted real friendly.

This Friday, as usual, Miss Eichelberger's father picked her up after school to take her home for the weekend. They stopped by the house to get her suitcase of clothes to launder. On Mondays, he would drop her suitcase off at our house and take her the rest of the way to school. When he learned that Esther had to go to Lititz every Monday morning, he offered to give her a lift since he was passing that way and was glad to help.

This Sunday brought the last night of the revival meetings. The church was packed and the message powerful. After the dismissal, I went back to where Franklin was standing. On the way I noticed, back a little farther, the two Miller boys having a discussion of some kind.

The younger one was tugging at the arm of his older brother Earl, who was my age. Earl seemed worried about something. I called Franklin's attention to what they were doing: "I bet Earl thinks he should go up to the preacher but is too timid."

"Maybe you ought to go and talk to them," Franklin said. So I did.

"I'm in trouble," Earl said. "I know I should go up there, but I don't know how." Then he told me his story. "Last month I almost died, and I'm still really weak." He had an attack of appendicitis, and before they got to the doctor, "My 'pendix busted, and they thought I wouldn't make it. I would'uv died without being in church. I gotta do something before the revival is over."

"I'll go up there with you," I offered, "and take you to the preacher if you want me to."

He was glad for that, and we walked up together. I introduced him to the preacher so Earl could get himself "straightened out."

I felt good. It was the first "missionary" kind of thing I had ever done. That evening when Franklin and I were talking about the meetings, he said, "Levi, you did something real good for the Miller boy. How did you notice them? What made you understand what it was all about? There were also a lot of other people around, just talking."

"It was easy for me," I replied, "because Earl looked just like I had felt when I was making up my mind."

Now it was Monday again. Everything was back to normal—at least so I thought. Then Miss Eichelberger came close to me when I was by myself and said in a low voice, "Well, Levi, now maybe you will behave yourself in school. I really hope so."

That's all she said, but it was enough. I was ashamed of the way I had been acting. For the first time, I realized that my "stand" would have to be more than just being a church member. How would I be able not to be one of the bunch of boys who always made trouble for the teacher? Maybe I was going to have to be one of the sissies. I knew there would be plenty to think about. I would have to talk to Franklin about it.

That evening Miss Eichelberger was her usual self. She didn't ever say anything to Mama about how I had acted at school. I was glad, because Mama would have told Dad, and he would have given me a spanking suitable for a twelve year old.

Miss Eichelberger just minded her own business. She didn't talk at the table; that was our time to talk. She established herself each evening at Dad's table-top desk and corrected papers or read books. Dad had to wait until Saturday to do his things at the desk. He used to write checks and handle other things like that in the evenings.

One day Mama gave me a Bible she had bought for me in town. It wasn't big like those the preachers had or like Dad's. Those Bibles had frills around the covers, and the edges of the sheets were shiny like gold. Mine was a child's Bible, as the title page claimed. It didn't have a lot of extra pages telling where to look for things like the Ten Commandments.

I got to like my little Bible. One of the first things I did was to look up John 3:16. That was also marked in the offprint of the Gospel of John that the Gideon lady had given us at school years ago. When I found the verse, I underscored the lines.

As a convert, I was determined to read my Bible regularly. I knew I would have to do so. Franklin had told me that was the only way to become free of my mean streak.

23

Physiognomy

This year, for the first time, Eva wouldn't be with us for Thanksgiving. She and Rube would be celebrating their Thanksgiving with his mother and his two sisters at their home in Lititz. That was to be expected, since that had been Rube's home for many years. But then we were also invited to share Thanksgiving with them. Mama said we had our own plans but that we would stop by in the afternoon for a short visit.

After stuffing ourselves up to the ears with our special dinner, we sat around while Mama and the girls did the dishes. Then all eight of us crowded into the car and drove to the Carpers' house in Lititz. Dad and Mama were in the front seat, with three-year-old Junior in the middle. The back seat was a bit crowded. Helen and Franklin sat on the outside, while Betty and Esther squeezed between them. I sat on the floor.

We often saw automobiles piled full of children. I remember once when such a carful came to visit us. The mother called to the back seat, "All right, girls, pile out." The door opened and children came bursting forth.

We arrived at the Carpers while we were still trying to digest our great feast. Ellen Carper received us at the door and led us directly into the dining room, where the table was set with all kinds of pies, cakes, and cookies. Dinner plates with silverware were in place, and glasses of lemonade were clustered at one end of the table.

"Why, look at this!" Mama exclaimed. "Isn't it nice? But you know we just had dinner."

"I know," said Ellen. "But let's just sit around the table to talk. Dessert is there if anybody wants some."

So we all sat down at the table to visit. The Carpers still living at home were Rube's widowed mother; his two older sisters, Lizzie and Ellen; and a sometime visitor, Uncle Gus. Conversation started slowly, with comments among the women about the good pies and cakes and recipes.

When the subject changed to questions about possible Carper relatives and ancestors, interest quickened. At this point, as if by common understanding, old Mrs. Carper took over. Everyone just listened. Rube didn't add any comment.

Mrs. Carper spoke with a gentle voice, expressing her words distinctly, and she was easily understood. She said that their family seemed to be widely scattered and had lost touch with each other. Then she named those of her family, all living in the area.

At home with her were her two daughters, Lizzie

and Ellen. Then there was Jacob (Jake) with his wife and children, with whom Eva had boarded. There was also Henry, with his wife and children. Then there was the youngest son, Reuben.

The Carper women seemed quite nice and kind. Their voices were not loud or demanding. As we left from our short visit, I had a feeling of kindness and satisfaction. I was sorry that they didn't have a lot of cousins as we did.

I also wondered why Rube didn't have the same kind of voice his mother and sisters had. He always talked with an edge in his voice, as though he wanted to start an argument. On the way home, we started to talk about that, but Dad told us to keep quiet. Rube was in our family, and we should respect him for Eva's sake. But I kept wondering why he hadn't pushed himself into the discussion or tried to talk about his trip out West.

When we got home and the evening chores were done, Franklin got his new book and sat down to read. The book's title was *Physiognomy*. The inside flyleaf introduced the book as an "insight into detecting character traits by facial features, either inherited or developed." He sat down to read with satisfaction. We now had our electric lights installed.

These lights meant more to me than I had expected. Shadowy corners were gone, along with their hints of ghosts. I no longer worried about stumbling with a lamp and starting a fire. The bedrooms each had only one wall-bracket light, but it was so much better than a kerosene lamp. The downstairs rooms had ceiling lights with fancy shades. The brightness of the lights made the whole house seem like a happier place. I was sorry Eva didn't have electricity where she was living.

Franklin liked to talk about his physiognomy book and was glad to have us read it. We began to discuss physiognomy the way we used to share ideas on handwriting styles. Reading about different faces was a lot more interesting than trying to figure out what various kinds of penmanship revealed about people's character. Its suggestions were interesting.

Eyes told a lot. There was a picture of the clear eye of a dove. Beside it, for comparison, was an artist's picture of a sweet young woman, also with clear blue eyes. Such eyes displayed natural virtue. For an illustration of the absence of virtue, the book displayed side by side the big puffy eye of a pig and the gluttonous eye of an old evil king. Eyes told a lot about people, claimed the book.

Facial wrinkles also had meaning. Washboard wrinkles on the forehead showed a lack of purpose, while straight, vertical creases between the eyebrows displayed courage. A picture of Napoleon was given to support that point.

What bothered me was what it said about eyebrows. Straight, level eyebrows showed purpose and strength, while arched brows were a sign of weakness. My eyebrows were arched, and it didn't take Esther long to point that out to me.

Franklin told me not to worry about it. One of the richest and most well-liked men we knew would have failed, according to that book on physiognomy. He had a wrinkled brow and arched eyebrows. Yet people said he had a hundred thousand dollars in the bank.

<u>24</u>

Skating

Cold weather came early this year. Before Christmas, Zartman's dam was frozen, ready for skating. Since I was twelve years old, Dad let me go skating in the evenings. It was fun because some of the boys from Webster School were usually there, too. We skated back and forth together or just stood around warming ourselves by the little campfires some of the people kept burning along the shore.

The skates I had just bought from a neighbor were much better than the rusty ones I had found in one of our sheds. The clamps were bigger and stronger, and they had ankle straps. When they were clamped to my shoes, they "stayed put." Some people had shoe skates—shoes with the blade attached to the shoe sole. They were best of all, but they cost a lot.

When the moon was full, a lot of people would come, but not all of them skated. Some just stood along the shore, watching and talking with friends. One man set up a little peanut and candy stand. He fixed up a small table with a sign: CANDY AND DRINKS. At his booth was a crate of bottled root beer, with a bottle opener on the table. Ice wasn't necessary to keep the drinks cold. The vendor kept a bonfire going behind the stand, and sales were good.

Soon after skating was really underway, something new and exciting happened. The three Sensensich brothers brought to the dam a power sled they had built by themselves. They had a shop and were known for their ability with tools. The sled was a neat platform with steel runners.

It was big enough to carry three people. Two of the people would sit up front on seats made from old chairs with the legs cut off. Right behind the chairs was room for the operator to stand. At the back edge of the platform, a sturdy frame held a motorcycle engine with a wooden propeller like those used on airplanes.

Every part of the sled was strong and neat. On each side of the platform, braces supporting the engine frame also served as safety bars for the passengers. The propeller was on the back of everything, designed to push the sled instead of pulling it.

Since the sled couldn't be steered or turned on the ice, it was fastened to a rope tied to a central pivot. The pivot was secured to a pipe driven through the ice into the ground under the water.

We watched the brothers give it a trial run. One of them sat up front, and another one stood at the operator's place. The third brother cranked up the propeller, and off it went! The rope stretched and the power sled really went, scooting around in a large circle.

It was a success. After it drifted to a stop, they made some adjustments and stood by to answer any questions from the crowd that had gathered. They said they were going to offer rides for twenty-five cents after everything was set up properly.

At the pivot pipe they attached a heavy plank to the rope. To the plank they fastened a naptha gas spotlight, to light up the sled as it circled. Then they set up a wooden box at what would be the starting point. The box had a cardboard sign: 25¢ PER SEAT, 5 ROUNDS.

Now they were ready to start. The first passengers were boys, till one of the young men had a bright idea. He took his girlfriend for a ride. Around they went, round and round. She was screaming and hugging him as they went.

The "ring around a rosey" (as it came to be called) was a success. From then on, there were many more rides with strong, noble men supporting their screaming girlfriends.

It was quite a while before we younger boys got a chance to ride. Clarence Weidman figured out how much money the Sensensich brothers might make in a week. He calculated that ten rides a night, at fifty cents for a couple, would equal five dollars. Six nights would bring in thirty dollars! "My goodness," Clarence said, "those guys could get rich!"

"Well," one of the others said, "what will they do in summer?"

The excitement and thrill of the ice sled gradually decreased, and the Sensensich brothers took it away. The only ones left skating on the dam were the regular boys from the community.

One evening when I was skating with the boys from Webster, one of them pulled a pack of cigarettes from his pocket. Boys below sixteen weren't usually allowed to smoke. John Zartman said his older brother let him have one of his packs. It was only about half full, so he said he could have it to "fool with" while he was skating.

John began passing the pack around, to share it with the rest of us. I didn't want one, but they insisted. After they had lit their cigarettes, one of them said, "Go on, Levi; smoking one cigarette won't matter. I bet your pop smoked when he was a boy."

So I let him put his match to my cigarette and took a puff. Then I skated off, making big circles on the ice till I came close to the shore, where I secretly threw it in the bushes.

Soon we all took off our skates and left, walking together along the bank to the road, laughing and joking in friendly conversation. Allen said to me, "Now, Levi, you can't say you never had a cigarette in your mouth."

I knew I hadn't really smoked; I had just kept it in my mouth until I threw it away. I wondered why so many people smoked. What little bit I had tasted wasn't anything to get excited about.

25

Franklin Goes to Bible School

This year Eva wasn't with us for Christmas. She and her husband had been invited to share Christmas with Rube's brother Jake and his family. But all the rest of us were home, and as usual we had a good time. Helen gave Esther *The Harvester*, a book by Gene Stratton-Porter. She also gave me a book with two stories by Robert Louis Stevenson, *Kidnapped* and *The Strange Case of Dr. Jekyll and Mr. Hyde*.

Those were our favorite authors. We had already read some of their novels. I was sure each of us would read both books. Helen gave Franklin two nice notebooks he could use while studying at his Six-Week Bible Term in Virginia, at EMS.

He would be leaving in about a week. I was going to miss him for two reasons. First, he wouldn't be here for our frequent discussions. Second, I would have to do his work while he was gone. Cleaning the stables was one of his jobs that I hated. It was hard work and smelly.

Feeding the cows and horses wasn't bad. It made me feel good to see the animals waiting at their troughs for their feed. When I scooped in their feed, they seemed to say "Thank you." The low sound as they chewed their feed seemed like an animal lullaby.

Franklin and I had a lot to talk about before he left. He showed me the study outlines of the courses he would be taking and the schedule of his classes. Franklin told about staying in a dormitory room with another man who was a stranger. He said, "I'm afraid my roommate might be somebody 'dumb,' or maybe a 'smartie' who would be hard to live with."

He wondered if there might be a problem with the meals. "Suppose they serve things I can't stand? But the good side is that I won't have to work for six weeks."

Then I got up my nerve and asked him a question that was a mystery to me. It was easier to talk about unusual things when it was dark and we were in our bedroom. I forced myself to ask the question, "Where do little babies come from?"

He waited awhile before answering, "Why don't you ask Mama? She ought to know."

"I would never ask Mama such a thing," I said.

I could almost see him smiling there in the dark as he responded: "I asked her about it one time, and she just said, 'Oh, we don't talk about such things; you'll find out what you need to know when you get older.'"

The conversation stopped there. Franklin was seventeen years old now. I bet he knew but just didn't want me to know.

Early in the morning, two days after New Year's Day, Franklin left for Virginia. Dad drove him to Lancaster, where he would catch a ride with the Mosemanns. Three of them were going to college there. We all said our good-byes, and he was off to Lancaster with his suitcase. He looked rather special with his new hat and overcoat.

As they drove away, Mama called after him, "Now, be sure to write and tell us how it's going."

When Franklin was gone, things began to feel spooky when I was alone at night. To begin with, the light in our bedroom was mounted on the wall farthest from the stairway. I had to feel my way up the steps in the dark to find my way to the light. I knew where it was, and I would run my hand up the wall and give the pull-chain switch a jerk. The light came on, and any ghosts lurking in the dark would vanish.

Then I got an idea. I told Mama what it was, and she said it was all right for me to try it. I planned to tie a cord to the pull chain on the light and run it through little pulleys and eyelets all the way to the foot of the stairs. I lost no time in getting cord and pulleys.

After attaching the cord to the pull chain, I designed a run across the ceiling over the bed, and then a right turn along the stairs to the door below. I tied a double knot at the lower end to act as a knob. It was a good idea and worked perfectly. I could even reach up and pull the cord while still in the safety of my bed.

With my new pull-switch arrangement, I began to read my new *Dr. Jekyll* book in bed. It was a little scary, so I was glad I didn't have to get out of bed to turn off the light.

We received our first letter from Franklin about a week after he left. He liked the school, and he had a nice young man from near Johnstown for a roommate. Breakfasts were not too bad, but he would have to get used to leaving the table still hungry. He said one of the boys told him that people usually ate more than they needed at home.

Franklin had two teachers from Pennsylvania, one from near Johnstown, and one from Lancaster County. I looked forward to his return home and the stories I would hear.

Working Away from Home

26

Radios Arrive

With Franklin gone, I began to read more in bed at night. I finished reading the Dr. Jekyll part of that book and switched over to *Kidnapped*. It didn't start out really exciting, so I often fell asleep and found the book lying on the bed in the morning. I decided to put it aside for a while and began thinking about my latest interest—radios. People were always talking about radios.

Radios had become a popular fad. There were stories about radios, pictures about them, and jokes about them. Sears & Roebuck had radios and radio parts in their catalogs. The boys' section in our youth magazine, *The Youth's Companion*, had an article explaining how they worked.

Radios were called sets, and people referred to a particular kind as a hookup. The Crosley set was supposed to be a good hookup. Most sets used headphones or, as they were often called, headsets. Big sets required a big A battery like those used in automobiles and also a B battery. If a loudspeaker was used instead of headsets, a C battery was needed to power it.

I read everything I could find about radios. A lot of boys were assembling their own sets and hookups. It all seemed impossible until I read an article about a set that didn't need batteries. All the parts necessary to build it could be bought for less than ten dollars. The parts were listed, but the article didn't say how to put the hookup together.

This radio was called a crystal set because it used a galena crystal to sort out the sounds in the ether waves that "roamed the skies." The galena crystal had sensitive spots that were contacted by a fine, stiff wire, "the cat's whisker." The idea worked; one of the big boys we knew in Lancaster made one. He could tune in and get station *KDKA* way out in Pittsburgh. I knew I would never stop trying until I could make one too.

The term *cat's whisker* became slang for anything cute or unusual. "Hey, that's sure the cat's whisker," might be an expected remark about a special fountain pen or even a flashy new necktie. Radio lingo pervaded daily conversation.

One of the radio bugs was bragging that he got Canada on his hookup. Another guys said, "That's nothing; I got Greece [grease] on my pants this morning." Then someone else said, "Yes, and I have Turkey on my plate."

Sometime in January, Miss Eichelberger came down with the gripp. It was something like the flu, and she would be out for at least two weeks. The school directors had to find a substitute right away. They knew Eva had her teacher's certificate and lived close by, so they asked her to fill the vacancy. After some discussion, Rube agreed, and she took the job.

She began at once, taking up where Miss Eichelberger had the schoolbooks marked. Things went smoothly. Eva knew many of the pupils because she had grown up in the neighborhood. The pupils also knew she was Helen's older sister. She taught a lot like Helen did. Eva gave us some special projects to do that weren't in the books—things just for the little ones and other things for the older students.

There was story time for the lower grades. She would go up to the blackboard with chalk and eraser. As she told the story, Eva would quickly illustrate it on the board with stick men and stick girls. As the story of "Little Johnny and Little Mary" went on, the scenes were quickly changed by erasing and redrawing. Sometimes there were stick doggies or kitties.

At story time, everyone began to stop what they were doing to watch and listen. Eva noticed it but didn't seem to mind.

The special thing for the big boys and girls was more like work. Every day Eva would put a big long division problem on the board. Everyone who had studied long division was asked to work out the problem and turn in the answer on a signed slip of paper. She put the problem on the board this way: $46,351 \div 241 = ?$ We were supposed to set down the problem on our tablet the usual way and try to get the right answer.

There were always some incorrect answers. Then one of the boys pointed out that I always seemed to be right. They whispered among themselves that Eva must be giving me the answers. When they confronted me, I told them that wasn't true, but that I had a special secret way of doing the problems. They didn't believe it and demanded that to make it fair, I should show them how. So I did.

This was my way: After putting the problem at the top of the page, I set about in advance multiplying the divisor by every digit from 2 through 9. That way, all I had to do was look down and select the proper numbers needed. It kept me from multiplying each time to find the correct number. They said it wasn't anything so special "like magic." They just did it a little differently.

Franklin's six-week study course was finally over, and he was back home. He unpacked his suitcase and gave Mama a bundle of laundry. Franklin shook out his suit, put it on a hanger, and hung it on its usual hook on the bedroom wall.

I was waiting to see what he had brought back in the big cardboard box. It was heavy and bound on all four sides with heavy twine. When he carried it in, he used the twine like a handle.

Finally he put it on the bed and cut the twine. He opened the box, and as I had expected, it was full of books and notebooks. I knew there would be a lot to talk about.

27

More Changes

In March I had my thirteenth birthday and became a teenager. Maybe now I would begin to get tall like some of the other boys. Perhaps I would soon be getting a razor and starting to shave. But looking in the mirror, I couldn't even see any fuzz. People often spoke about boys "chasing their first whisker" when they were fifteen, more or less. Or when one of the boys was big and husky they might say, "Why, he began shaving at fourteen a'ready." I knew my shaving was far in the future.

As April approached, people began talking about daylight saving time. Back in 1918, toward the close of the war, the government had made a law that at a certain date in spring, everyone had to set their clocks forward one hour to save daylight. It was a waste of time to stay in bed when the sun was up.

There was a lot of argument about it, so the law was canceled the next year. But the idea didn't die.

During the summer, some big cities still had day-light saving time. The farmers didn't need it; they always got up early in the summer anyhow. The city folks liked it more, because they worked at jobs and it gave them more daylight hours in the evening after work. Some of the old-timers took a religious view and called regular time God's time, and day-light saving time man's time.

I was interested in growing up and developing big muscles in my forearms like Atlas. Pictures in advertisements showed him with great bulging muscles, lifting huge weights. Franklin fixed an old fork handle across some beams in the pig stable, to use for chinning exercises.

He practiced to where he could chin the bar six-teen times; his goal was to reach twenty-five. My limit was ten, but I was going to try to go up to twen-ty. Both of us were thin, and that helped. Heavy peo-ple had a lot of extra weight to pull up.

As we worked together around the barn and greenhouse, Franklin told me about his studies. He learned a lot about the history of the children of Israel in Egypt and about great Pharaoh Ramses. His studies on the apostle Paul and his journeys and imprisonment, made me think about how easy life was for us today.

I began to read my Bible more and to underscore certain verses like Franklin did. Now for the first time, I began to realize that the Bible should be stud-ied like a textbook to understand what it says.

Summertime was coming, with all its activities, swimming, fishing, and plenty of work, but no school. I was now at the stage where I could harness and work the horses. Steady black Tom was the lead horse, and Flory the gentle mare. We always wanted to have three horses, like some of the neighbors, but Dad didn't agree.

"We should just work our team steady," Dad said, "and be sure to water and feed them properly, according to the weather and amount of work." Five-minute rest periods in hot weather were also necessary. "Don't try to make two horses do three horses' work" was his rule.

Swimming was getting more interesting since we had begun to study different diving forms and swimming strokes last summer. This year I planned to learn how to swim like a professional. I borrowed Franklin's swimming book and read again about the crawl stroke, sidestroke, and breaststroke.

He had learned these strokes rather well, but I still just used the doggie paddle, trying to hold my entire head out of the water. Franklin told me, "Until you stop being afraid of getting your eyes under the water, you'll never be able to swim properly." This summer I was determined to overcome that problem.

Diving was another matter. Franklin was trying the swan dive, stretching his arms out like a bird and then bringing them together for the plunge. The jackknife meant jumping high, doubling up, and finally straightening for a neat entry into the water. The diving board was not high enough to properly complete either, but he kept trying.

My dives were not real dives. They were belly floppers. I was afraid to take a good, clean, headfirst plunge.

I wasn't interested in my little house down in the woods any more, and Betty took over my woodland domain. On Sundays when some of her seven-year-old friends came to visit, I could see them roaming by the stream and among the trees. Betty had many friends: Miriam Grube at school and Anna Mae Charles at Sunday school were special. She always seemed to be having a good time. I never saw her having an argument or disagreement.

One day Eva and Dad were talking together about my school for next year. I was in the top reader at Webster, and any more time there would simply be repeating the same books. It was time for me to go on to eighth grade at Lititz, as Esther had done, but I would have to take a qualifying examination. That's what Eva was talking about with Dad. The exams were standard and would be given at a certain time and place in Lititz.

I was excited about going to a big school again, but I was afraid of what would happen if I didn't pass the entry test. Everybody at Webster would know it and make fun of me. There was no way out; I had to keep calm and just do my best. The test was still a month away.

Meanwhile, I would study and review the hard arithmetic problems and history dates. Eva said the questions wouldn't be hard. They would be taken from the same books I had studied during the last years at Webster. "You should brush up on your spelling and rules of grammar," she suggested.

My interest in radio was not totally forgotten. I had a big cardboard box where I put the things I was accumulating to build my crystal set next winter. I had found the right size of oatmeal box to wrap my tuning coil around. I had also obtained a roll of the right gauge of coil wire at Trimmers for fifty cents. But the radio project was on hold. Summer was no time for radio. More important things were in store.

28

Vacation?

The last two weeks of school were easy and relaxed. Our lessons were simply a review of things we had already studied. Miss Eichelberger didn't seem to have much interest in what was going on, and we didn't even need to turn in any papers.

At recess, there were no games; we just stood around talking. Some of the big boys began to wear hats instead of their usual caps, and some of the girls wore thin frilly dresses. To be a part of the holiday spirit, I decided to wear my Sunday strawhat to school. I tried to sneak out the side door with it, but Mama saw me and made me put it back.

Two Saturdays before school closed, I had to take my eighth-grade entry test. Forry Zartman was also taking it, so Dad drove us to Lititz, where the test was to be given. It would begin at nine o'clock and finish at eleven. We had been instructed to bring our own pencils but nothing else that might be used to help with the test. Dad said he would be back again at eleven to take us home.

Shortly before nine, as we were waiting at our desks, a well-dressed man entered and introduced himself. He said he was assigned to conduct the test and proceeded to lay down the rules. There would be no whispering to others during the test period. Anyone seen trying to copy from someone else's paper would be given a zero for the whole test.

He gave each of us a small pack of plain white paper to use in answering our test questions. Next he handed us the test questions, laying them face down on each desk. Looking at the wall clock, he said, "Well, it's now ten minutes till nine. Let me explain the scope of your tests."

I didn't know what *scope* meant, but I soon found out. He said there were three subjects: arithmetic, history, and grammar. Our ability to spell and write would be judged by how well we wrote our test answers. Then he looked at the clock again and said, "Turn over your test papers and begin."

Everyone seemed scared. I could hear the faint shuffling of papers and an occasional nervous cough. Several times I coughed, too. This was the first time I ever had taken a big test, and it made me nervous and shaky.

One of the questions in the grammar test was strange to me, not like any of the questions in our grammar book. Just then, a girl from another school raised her hand. The instructor recognized her and asked her to stand and give her name and her school. She did so, and he asked, "Do you have a question about the test?"

"Yes."

"Now you may state your question in a voice that all may hear," he said.

By that time, she seemed to be getting nervous, but she stated her question in a clear voice. It was the same one I was wondering about.

He thanked her for bringing it to his attention and carefully explained it so we could understand it better. Then, like an army man, he said, "All of you have now heard the question and its explanation. You may now resume your work."

The girl who had remained standing all the while finally sat down.

As we continued our work, it happened that Forry Zartman, sitting next to me, laid one of his finished papers face down on my pile of plain paper. I didn't notice and began writing my test on its blank side. Forry finally saw it and began to punch me and point at the paper.

When I saw his excitement, I turned the paper over and saw his writing on the other side. One of us would have to do that sheet over again. I didn't give up, so he patiently rewrote his work. I felt badly, but after all, it was his fault. I scratched over his writing and turned the sheet in with my other test papers. I think the instructor saw it happen and understood because he didn't say anything about it. At eleven o'clock, the test was over for better or worse.

By the time school was over at Webster, we had received the results of my test in an official-looking envelope. It contained a short letter of congratulations. Included in the envelope was a certificate stating that I had successfully completed my first seven years of elementary school. I felt like shouting! Now, no more Webster and on to Lititz.

Summer was going to be special this year. Maybe we would be having a family picnic in August along the Conestoga, like we did two years ago. I knew Franklin was planning to buy a lot of fireworks from the Blazzel catalog again. There would be a lot of fun this Fourth of July—all kinds of firecrackers, sparklers, and Roman candles. He said he was going to get some skyrockets, too. The advertisements in the catalog said, "Celebrate the 4th the Blazzel way."

There were special things I was looking forward to. One of them was finally to get some real grown-up overalls. So far, mine had been the boy's sizes, with only one hip pocket and two small side pockets. The adult overalls had two big hip pockets, and the side pockets were large and roomy. The bib had a watch and pencil pocket, and on the right pant leg was a narrow pocket for a folded carpenter's rule. The left pant leg had a loop to hold a hammer.

Franklin had worn overalls like that since he was thirteen, so I guessed it was time for me to have them, too. I knew Mama could be persuaded, because the ones I had now were rather well worn. Then too, I was going to buy a big new pocketknife with a lot of blades. My present one had only one blade because the other had broken off. Dad would be paying me again this summer, and I could buy some other things too, like fishhooks and sinkers.

Life was good. I watched little Junior fooling around with our family dog, Baggy, who liked to play. If we slapped our leg and said, "Baggy, go get it," he would run around barking, looking for something, and return panting as though he had just caught a terrible lion.

Junior would pat his head, ruffle his shag hair, and say, "Good dog, Baggy."

Esther adapted a line from the Declaration of Independence to express our association with Baggy: "We are endowed with the rights to life, liberty, and the pursuit of Baggy."

School was out, and I was going to be working with the horses again, wearing my new overalls. I even thought about buying myself an Ingersoll Yankee pocket watch to carry in the watch pocket. They only cost one dollar each.

I was planning how to ask Mama about getting my new overalls when Dad came to me and said, "Boy, I'm going to send you to live at Eva's this summer, to give them some help."

I was shocked speechless. "Why?" I finally asked.

"You aren't needed at home, and Eva could use a little help."

I started bawling and promised to work hard and not be lazy if I could stay home—but he didn't budge. I asked Franklin about it, and he wasn't much help: "When Dad gets a notion, he never changes his mind."

I tried to talk to Mama about it, and she just agreed with Dad. I might have expected it; she always took Dad's advice. When I asked her about new overalls, she said my old ones would do for another year. I was getting nowhere. No one seemed to care much about me. I didn't ask Esther's advice, thinking she had nothing to offer that would help.

It was Saturday when Dad gave me the bad news,

and I was to leave home on Monday morning. I looked down at my half-worn-out overalls; they were too small and had a patch on one knee. I didn't have to be told that I wouldn't be earning money this summer. Eva didn't have any, and I knew Rube wasn't about to pay me anything.

I felt totally rejected and cast out of the family. There would be no Conestoga picnic and no great Fourth-of-July firecrackers for me.

What hurt most was the way Dad said, "You aren't needed at home." Also, to be away from all the things we enjoyed together was almost more than I could stand. Crying didn't help. Dad was the silent type. He thought suffering made people strong. I had heard him say that once when he was giving his little Sunday school opening talk.

I was stuck fast in a situation that I would have to try to live with. There was one thing that would help: Eva had always been my special friend when I was in trouble.

29

Day One

On Sunday afternoon Mama got an old suitcase from the attic and began packing some clothes for me to take along to Eva's. She opened it, laid it on my bed, and began selecting things from the dresser.

For my everyday clothes, there were an extra pair of overalls and several shirts plus some BVDs (the name of men's underwear). She also sent along a change of school clothes in case they wanted to take me along to town sometime.

My Sunday clothes remained at home. I was supposed to be at home on Sunday and go to our church. Eva and Rube didn't go to Sunday school; they went to church services where Rube used to attend. When Mama was through with the packing, she asked, "Do you want to add anything?"

I was going to say no, but then I remembered my Bible. I laid it on top of the clothes. Mama closed the lid and snapped the clasps.

After breakfast on Monday morning, Dad started the car and said, "Come on, Boy. I'm driving you to Eva's."

I shoved the suitcase on the backseat and sat

down beside it. It wasn't far to Eva's, only about a twenty-minute drive. As we wound along the narrow country road, none of us said anything. I guess there was nothing to say.

When we got there, Dad stopped in front of the house, and I climbed out with my suitcase. Dad said, "Now behave yourself and do what they tell you." After that directive, he turned the car around and drove away, leaving me standing at the front gate.

Eva saw me from the kitchen window and came out to meet me. She took me inside and thanked me for offering to help them this summer. She was just finishing washing the breakfast dishes, and Rube was out in the barn. She took my suitcase and told me to follow her upstairs to my room.

I began feeling a lot better. She made it seem as though I was being kind to them. Eva always had a way of making people feel good.

She said I should just leave the suitcase on the floor. In the evening after the farmwork, she would help me arrange things. We went downstairs. She stayed in the kitchen to finish the dishes, and I went out to find Rube. He was putting the harness on a horse named Dan. My first job was going to be riding and steering Dan while Rube handled a single-horse cultivator in the cornfield.

Neither of Rube's two horses had been taught the single or jerk line. At home, Old Tom would turn by the driver's signal of "Gee" (right) or "Haw" (left), or a pull or jerk of the single line. We went right to work in the field. I was doing something helpful that was familiar to me. I knew as much about it as Rube did.

At noon we unhooked and took the horse to the

barn, gave him water, and put him in the stable. Rube showed me how to feed the horses. He gave them oats, though we fed ours corn. Then we went to the house for dinner. Eva was a good cook. I had never tasted her cooking before because she was always going to school or teaching school.

The afternoon went just like the morning. We continued cultivating, and by evening we were through with the field. Back at the barn, we gave the horse a drink at the trough and put him in the stable. After taking off the harness, Rube began to show and tell me how to do the morning and evening chores.

He assigned me to feed and bed the horses and Bessie the cow. I was supposed to milk Bessie right after breakfast and right after supper. By then, I could milk a cow but not very well. Mama always did the milking at home. So after supper this evening, I was supposed to milk old Bessie. I hoped she wasn't a kicker.

After finishing with the evening milking, it was still daylight. When Eva had finished washing the supper dishes, she took me up to my room and helped me get things straightened out.

She said, "We call this Reuben's room because everything in it came from his home, but that doesn't mean everything in the room belonged only to him. His family gave us the bed and covers from their home. The chest of drawers is his, and the things on the wall are his. Here, the top drawer is empty. You can use it for your clothes."

Then she left me to do my own unpacking. I put my clothes in the drawer with the school things on the bottom. My school shoes went on the floor by the chest. I laid my Bible on the windowsill.

There, by myself, I looked over the room again. It reminded me of Rube. I could almost see him sitting as a child on the little Grannie chair in the corner. I guess what triggered it was what I saw on the wall. There, stretched out, was a cloth pennant with the words, "WENATCHEE Wn." That was where he and his boy friends had gone to pick apples in the state of Washington. It was the subject of his oft-repeated story.

Right below it was a little shelf held up with brackets. On it a single book was lying, *Tom Swift and His Motorcycle.* By this time, it was getting a little too dark to read, but I looked at it anyway. The back fly-leaf had a list of other Tom Swift books. There were also a few pictures of motorcycle situations.

It came to me all over again. This room was Rube, pure and simple: his big story, his entire library, and echoes of his life in the bed and chest.

I was tired and just went to bed. My first day at Eva's was closing, and I was homesick. A picture of the family at home came to my mind. Dad would be sitting on his chair near the light, reading the paper. Franklin would be reading one of his books, and Esther would probably be talking to Betty about something that happened at Lititz.

I could see Junior on the floor with a favorite toy, and Mama would be sitting on the rocker with her sewing basket on her lap, mending clothes. Helen wouldn't be there because she was at Pennsylvania State College, taking a summer course on library work. She had been promised a position in the library at the University of Pennsylvania in Philadelphia.

I was lonesome, but my weariness soon took over, and I was asleep.

30

That Long Summer

Eva and Rube were both nice to me. Once when I was telling about Franklin's tackle box and how we went fishing, Rube gave me the square tin lunch box he had used when he worked at Lititz. He said I could fix it up like a tackle box. Following his suggestion, I installed some partitions, using strips of wood I found in the tobacco shed. It made a neat tackle box, but I didn't have any tackle.

After a few days had passed, Rube told me Eva needed me to help her a bit around the house. My work schedule was outlined. Milking and caring for Bessie was my job. Also, I was to hoe and weed the garden patch below the barn and tobacco shed, beside the road. I would be caring for rows of squash, peas, and beans. Eva would tell me how to help around the house.

There were several things here at Eva's that were interesting to me. One was Rube's hound, Duke. He never ran around and barked like Baggy did. He just followed along wherever I went and laid down near my work site.

The other interesting thing was the friendly neighbors, Mr. and Mrs. Shearer, who lived within shouting distance up the road. They often stopped by for short visits in the evening. Since they were traditional Swiss Germans, their English conversation was strongly flavored with German pronunciation and word order.

They knew a lot of things I had never heard about. Mrs. Shearer went with Eva to the old herb and tea patch in the yard beside Carper's house. She pointed out a number of the stalks that were remedies for special ailments. There was the *Alte Frau,* a tea especially for old women's aches and pains. Another one was the *Alte Mann,* good for old men.

Eva tried the *Alte* teas, but they were too bitter. She laughed and said, "I'm glad we aren't old."

Hiram (Mr. Shearer) liked to talk about the proper time for planting according to the phase of the moon. He and his wife both had a certain "gift" of powwowing to cure various ills. He told how one of his horses hurt its leg and was quickly healed by powwowing. He claimed that warts could be easily removed by this method. They both offered to powwow for any of us if we needed it.

He also had a way of foretelling the weather by certain signs in nature. According to him, "This summer there will be a lot of severe thunderstorms."

One evening when Hiram had stopped by, Rube told him, "The groundhogs have begun to strip some of the ears off the early sweet corn."

"If you know where the groundhog hole is," Hiram said, "you could try to drown him out with water."

"There's a hole right below the tobacco shed," I reported. Sure enough, when we looked, it was a hole that showed signs of being used currently.

Hiram offered to help, and we set about the project. Rube laid his gun close by, and we each began pouring buckets of water in the hole. Duke stood by as though he knew what was going on.

Finally the hole was full, and the old groundhog pushed his head into view. Duke saw the groundhog and tried to grab it. The groundhog responded by clawing Duke's nose. With a loud yelp, Duke withdrew to a safe distance. Then Rube took his gun and shot the groundhog. I grabbed one leg and dragged it down to the meadow for the buzzards.

Just as Hiram had said, we began to have bad thunderstorms. At home, thunderstorms never scared me. But now, away from the refuge of home, I began trembling with fear when I heard the distant rumble of thunder and saw black clouds on the horizon. The storm closed over us with sharp cracks of lightning, followed by booms of thunder that shook the house.

Meanwhile, I would get my little Bible and try to read it for security. People said that for special help from the Bible, one should set it upright on the table and let it to open at random. The page that appeared was supposed to have a special message for that moment. My Bible would always open at the same place, Colossians 3: "If ye then be risen with Christ, seek those things which are above. . . ."

I didn't know what the text meant. I just sat there trembling, reading the same words over and over. When the storm went by, I closed the Bible and went out of the house, once more free and alive.

My daily routine wasn't demanding; I would have worked much harder at home. But my feeling of rejection still hung on. As each evening settled in and we wound up evening chores, an old familiar song would come to my mind:

> Twilight is stealing over the sea,
> Shadows are falling dark on the lea;
> Borne on the night winds, voices of yore
> Come from that far-off shore. (A. S. Kieffer)

My family at home, gathering together after supper, always came to my mind. I wanted to be with them.

Every Saturday afternoon I would walk home. It didn't take long, maybe a little less than an hour. It seemed strange to me, but my fear of dogs returned again. So instead of following the easy roads where dogs might be, I cut across fields. I made an excuse for myself, thinking it shortened my way, but the opposite was true.

This year the Fourth of July was on Friday. In the evening after dark, I looked toward Lititz to see the skyrocket displays at the carnival for Independence Day. At home, we could always enjoy the brilliant rockets exploding all over the sky. But Lititz was so far away that I couldn't see them from the Carpers. On Saturday I was sure I would hear about it. Maybe Franklin would still have some of his own firecrackers left.

I learned that my family had watched the rocket displays, but Franklin's fireworks were all used up. He said he hadn't really spent a lot of money on them this year. The six Roman candles and several dozen firecrackers were all gone.

While we were talking and they were bringing me up to date on the week's activities, Esther gave me one of her cute, sly looks. She grinned slightly and said, "Well, if we have enough thunderstorms, you should soon have read most of the Bible."

That comment was like a punch in my stomach. I knew that if Eva had quietly told Mama, it would have been out of sympathy and not so Esther could make fun of me.

On Sunday evening I changed my clothes and was ready for Dad to drop me off at Eva's place. Then Mama pulled me aside and said to me in a special way, "Eva and Rube will be getting a baby this summer."

All the things I had wondered about babies were back again. This time I would be alone with my questions. I didn't know what to think or do. As Dad quietly drove me back to the Carpers, the last verse of "Twilight Is Stealing" came to my mind. It had nothing to do with anything that was happening, but it just kept going over in my mind.

Voices of loved ones, songs of the past!
Still linger 'round me, while life shall last.
Lonely I wander, sadly I roam,
Seeking that far-off home.
—A. S. Kieffer

31

The Baby Mystery

Eva began to use me more about the house. I swept the porch, brought things up from the cellar, and emptied the slop bucket. That wasn't unusual since I sometimes did the same things at home. My regular work kept me busy, especially on those days when I helped with the hay and wheat.

I kept thinking about little babies. Down in Virginia, Mama had come home from the hospital carrying Little Betty. Later, after a stay in the hospital at Lancaster, she had come home with Junior. The old stories about storks bringing babies or finding them in the cabbage patch were nonsense. I knew doorstep babies were put there by someone who wanted to give them away.

A remark I had overheard added to my confusion. Once I was going into the church just as two young women met. One of them had a tiny baby in her arms. The other one smiled and said, "Why

Alice, how nice! Where did you find that sweet little thing?"

Alice chuckled a little and replied, "In the dresser drawer, of course." She said it as though it was a joke, but I wasn't sure.

Eva was spending more time up in her bedroom. Sometimes I heard her up there, running her sewing machine. She was probably making clothes for their soon-expected baby. I finally stopped trying to solve the mystery I couldn't understand. Nothing made sense to me.

About two weeks after the Fourth, Rube said, "I'm going to give you an extra day off because you've been so helpful lately. You can go home on Friday instead of Saturday this week."

I was glad because maybe I could go swimming again on Saturday afternoon. Also, I could go to Young Peoples Meeting in the evening and see some of my friends.

Sunday school and church services were as usual, and our dinner that followed was especially good. Right after dinner, the phone rang out in the kitchen. Mama left the table as though she had been expecting a call. When she returned, she looked excited and said, "It's a little girl!"

It wasn't hard for me to guess what she meant. Eva and Rube had "gotten" their baby.

My weekend schedule changed. Dad said we should just settle down while he and Mama went to see how things were with Eva and the baby. Several hours later they returned with the good news that their first grandchild was a little girl named Ruth.

"Rube's sister Ellen will be staying to help in the

house for awhile," Dad said. "On Monday evening we'll all go out to visit them."

When Monday evening came, we crawled into the car and went for the visit. Ellen met us at the door, and Rube was right behind with a proud smile on his face. We went indoors and found chairs in the living room, but Eva and the baby weren't there.

When we were all settled in our chairs, Ellen said, "Well, I'll go upstairs and see if Eva is ready." In a few minutes she was down again. Everything was all right, and we all filed up the steps. There was Eva in bed with little bitty Ruth snuggled beside her. It reminded me of the time I had seen little Henry Jr. there in the hospital bed with Mama.

We stood around the bed awhile, chitchatting about whether Ruth looked more like Eva's family or Rube's. We didn't stay long and were soon ready to leave. I followed along to the car, expecting to go home again, assuming that Ellen would be taking my place. But when I started to get in the car, Dad didn't allow it. I tried to force myself in over his objections, but to no avail.

"You have to stay here and help for the rest of the summer," Dad said.

I returned to the house, wiping tears from my eyes. Back in the house, Rube and Ellen were conversing in the living room. I would still have my same room. Ellen was using the third bedroom, which had been made ready for her. Now I knew the sounds I had heard upstairs had been more than Eva's sewing machine. She had also been getting things ready for Ellen.

I also realized that the older ones had been

preparing things for some time. That's why Ellen seemed to know where everything was and what had to be done. I was tired and gloomy, so I went on up to bed, falling asleep while Rube and Ellen were still downstairs.

In the morning, I got up as usual, not knowing what to expect. But there was no need for me to worry. Ellen was there in full command, with breakfast on the table. "Good morning, Levi," she said. "I was just about to call you. Didn't you sleep a little late?"

We ate mostly in silence. Ellen remarked that Eva looked well and the baby seemed to have a good appetite.

Ellen took full control of the household affairs. My help was no longer needed around the house. She would be looking after things as long as Eva was upstairs. Ellen always referred to Eva in her present situation as being "upstairs." For me, she just said "going to bed" or "sleeping late." After a few weeks, she said, "I'll be leaving several days after Eva is downstairs again." The terms "upstairs" and "downstairs" took on mysterious meaning, like some form of control.

As Ellen had said, she went home to Lititz after Eva had been downstairs several days. Little Ruth added a lot of life to the household. I felt more like I was at home when I heard the baby crying and Eva and Rube talking to it in baby talk. I wasn't quite as homesick any more, and thunderstorms seemed less fierce. Also, I could count how many days were left until I would be home again. I still had a little fear of strange dogs.

During my days at Eva's, I became aware that money was scarce. There wasn't much on the farm to sell. The sweet corn crop was good, but there wasn't much of it. The potatoes wouldn't be ready for awhile. At home, there was always something to sell—eggs, butter, or market crops. Of course, they had only been on the farm a little over a year.

One day Rube told Eva, "I'm going to try to get a job at the silk mill on the night shift. I know the foreman, and I'm going to see him about it."

Eva agreed. He planned to go and apply for a job on Wednesday night. He had talked with Eva about it, and they both agreed that calling on the phone would not be the best way to apply for the job.

On Wednesday evening, Rube surprised me by saying I was to go along. I had no idea how that would help, but I didn't mind. I got into my school clothes and went along to the mill.

When we got there, Rube said, "Well, let's go on in and see what happens." He seemed a little scared when he saw the uniformed watchman. "I've come to see the foreman," Rube told him. It was no problem. The guard just went off down the aisles between the looms to get the man.

I had never been inside a silk mill or knitting mill. I knew a bit about them, because people we knew worked there. At night the lights over the looms were a soft green instead of clear and bright. That was supposed to protect the sight of the workers. When we passed close to the mills, we could hear the hum of looms inside. Now as we stood waiting, I could experience it from the inside.

When the man finally came, he and Rube stepped

aside and talked together for awhile. The sound of the looms kept me from hearing their conversation. When they finished talking, Rube came to me, and we went out to the car. He didn't get the job.

The end of summer was near, and I was glad. I had one last, special job to do. Dan, the horse, needed to have his left back shoe replaced because it was loose. I got on his back and rode him out toward Clay, to the blacksmith. When I told him what I wanted, he looked at the horse and asked, "Is he a kicker?"

"No, he isn't."

He walked around the horse several times and asked again, "Are you sure he doesn't kick?" Finally, taking all precautions, he went about replacing the shoe. When he was finished, I took Dan to a big square sandstone used as a mounting step, hopped on the saddle, and rode home to Eva's.

That was my last special job. August ended on Sunday. I would be going home on Saturday, in just two more days.

<u>32</u>

Looking Ahead

Since I had passed the eighth-grade entrance test, Eva seemed to be worried about my big jump from little one-room Webster to the big village school at Lititz. She told me not to be "pushy" around the school ground and to always pay attention in my classes.

Eva suggested that since Webster would be starting two weeks before Lititz, maybe I should go there for two weeks to get me "on track." She dug up an old German saying to emphasize her advice: "*In Roi zu schtelle* (to put me in the row, admonish me)." When I first began to plow with horses, Dad would start me in the row.

However, we soon heard that Tommy Wolf would be teaching at Webster. So we dropped the idea of me attending there for two weeks.

During that long summer vacation, I think Eva was glad to have me around. Although she spoke perfect, unaffected English, she enjoyed explaining old German sayings to me. One of them was about "a lazy schoolboy, a *verdarewe Bu* (a spoiled brat)." There were many others. I enjoyed hearing them. Conversations between big sister and little brother from time to time did something for both of us.

During those last days before school, I had some worries. I thought deeply about the things Eva had said to me. I had learned a lot the hard way.

Among the things I remembered most were the "*verdarewe Bu*" and the saying "*in Roi zu schtelle.*" Eva helped me get over being a spoiled brat, and she was the most effective way I could have been "*schtelled*" in the "*Roi.*"

Old memories bounced around in my mind as I looked forward to the future. But, like I had heard so many times, "Take care of the present, and the future will take care of itself." It was up to me.

The Author

Levi B. Weber, Newport News, Virginia, is a retired building contractor, real estate developer, and broker. For eighteen years, Weber produced the Rock of Ages radio broadcast and directed the chorus for it.

Levi and his wife June are members of the Warwick River Mennonite Church. He has actively served in the congregation, Virginia Mennonite Conference, Mennonite Economic Development Associates, Mennonite Development Associates, and on the boards of Eastern Mennonite College and Mennowood Retirement Community.